BACKPACKING IN MICHIGAN

Second Edition

Pat Allen
and
Gerald L. DeRuiter

D1315318

Ann Arbor *The University of Michigan Press*

Second Edition 1989
Copyright © by the University of Michigan 1982, 1989
All rights reserved
Published in the United States of America by
The University of Michigan Press
Manufactured in the United States of America

1996   1995   *7   6*

Trail maps have been redrawn from state
and federal maps provided by the
courtesy of the Michigan Department of
Natural Resources, the United States
Forest Service, and the National Park
Service.

Library of Congress Cataloging-in-Publication Data

Allen, Pat, 1938–
  Backpacking in Michigan.

  Bibliography: p.
  1. Backpacking—Michigan—Guide-books. 2. Michigan—
Description and travel—1981–   —Guide-books.
I. De Ruiter, Gerald, 1950–   . II. Title.
GV199.42.M5A44 1989   917.74   88-27753
ISBN 0-472-06386-3

The civilized man has built a coach,
but he has lost the use of his feet.

Ralph Waldo Emerson

Preface to the Second Edition

We are excited about this second edition. In its preparation, we have explored many miles of new trails. We have updated some of the earlier trail descriptions and we have included three remote wilderness areas for experienced backpackers to explore. Most of the North Country National Scenic Trail sections through the national forests have now been completed and are waiting for your discovery. In the earlier edition they were only "proposed" trails.

For those of you who are part of the boom in fitness walking, this second edition contains information to help you use some of the trails for walking vacations. Information on hiking and health will help others get in shape to backpack.

We know from talking to our readers that some of you return again and again to the same favorite area. Others of you have gone through the book trying different trails in succession. You will find much to enjoy in this new edition. We wish you good hiking.

Acknowledgments

We are indebted to those individuals and groups who have preserved natural places and those who have created pathways through them. We are grateful to our hiking companions who have so enriched the experience for us. We thankfully acknowledge the significant assistance of the personnel of the Michigan Department of Natural Resources, the United States Forest Service, and the National Park Service.

Contents

Michigan
Trails

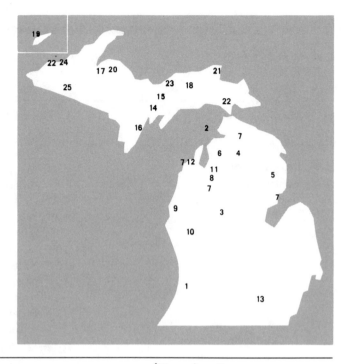

TRAIL	TRAIL DIFFICULTY	TRAIL LENGTH (IN MILES)	TRAIL TIME (IN DAYS)	BEST SEASON	WILDERNESS EXPERIENCE	FEE/PERMIT	GOVERNING AGENCY	CHILDREN UNDER 12	MAP PAGE
1. Allegan	Easy	18	2	Apr.–mid-Oct.	No	Yes	DNR	Yes	147–48
2. Beaver Island	Easy	6+	2–3	Apr.–mid-Oct.	No	Yes	DNR	Yes	149
3. Green Pine Lake	Mod.	11	2	June–mid-Oct.	No	Yes	DNR	Yes	150
4. High Country	Mod. to diff.	50+	7+	June–mid-Oct.	Yes	Yes	DNR	No	151–53
Shingle Mill	Mod.	6–11	1–3	Apr.–mid-Oct.	No	Yes	DNR	Yes	152
Clear Lake–Jackson Lake	Easy	7.7	2	Apr.–mid-Oct.	No	Yes	DNR	Yes	152
Sinkholes	Mod.	1.5	—	Apr.–mid-Oct.	No	Yes	DNR	Yes	153
5. Hoist Lakes	Mod.	20	3	All year	Yes	No	Hur.–Man. N.F.	Yes	154
6. Jordan River	Mod.	18	2–3	June–mid-Oct.	No	Yes	DNR	No	155
7. Shore to Shore	Easy to mod.	219+	—	Apr.–mid-Oct.	No	Yes	DNR/Hur. N.F.	Yes	156
N. Spur	Easy	86	4–5	Apr.–mid-Oct.	No	Yes	DNR	Yes	—
S. Spur	Easy	44	4–5	Apr.–mid-Oct.	No	Yes	DNR	Yes	—
8. Muncie Lakes	Easy	9	2	All year	No	Yes	DNR	Yes	157

TRAIL	TRAIL DIFFICULTY	TRAIL LENGTH (IN MILES)	TRAIL TIME (IN DAYS)	BEST SEASON*	WILDERNESS EXPERIENCE	FEE/PERMIT	GOVERNING AGENCY	CHILDREN UNDER 12	MAP PAGE
9. Nordhouse Dunes	Mod.	10+	2–3	All year	Yes	No	Hur.-Man. N.F.	Yes	158
10. North Country	Easy to mod.	400+†	30	All year	Yes	No	Multi	Yes	159–62
White Cloud	Easy	26.9	3–4	All year*	No	No	Hur.-Man. N.F.	Yes	160
Baldwin	Mod.	10	2–3	Apr.–mid-Oct.	No	No	Hur.-Man. N.F.	Yes	161
Manistee	Mod.	20.2	2–3	Apr.–mid-Oct.	No	No	Hur.-Man. N.F.	Yes	162
11. Sand Lakes	Easy	15	2–3	All year	No	Yes	DNR	Yes	163
12. Sleeping Bear Dunes	Easy	5 short loops	2–3	All year	No	Yes	Nat. Pk. Ser.	Yes	164–67
Platte Plains	Easy to mod.	10	2–3	All year	No	Yes	Nat. Pk. Ser.	Yes	165
N. Manitou Island	Diff.	—	2–3	Apr.–mid-Oct.	Yes	Yes	Nat. Pk. Ser.	Yes	166
S. Manitou Island	Easy	—	2–3	Apr.–mid-Oct.	No	Yes	Nat. Pk. Ser.	Yes	167
13. Waterloo-Pinckney	Mod.	46	5	Apr.–mid-Oct.	No	Yes	DNR	Yes	168
14. Bay de Noc–Grand Island	Mod.	40	4–5	Apr.–mid-Oct.	No	No	Hia. N.F.	No	171
15. Bruno's Run	Mod.	7.25	2	All year	No	Yes	Hia. N.F.	Yes	172
16. Cedar River	Easy to mod.	2–7	2	All year	No	Yes	DNR	Yes	173
17. Craig Lake	Mod. to diff.	10+	1–5	June–Sept.	Yes	Yes	DNR	No	174
18. Fox River	Mod. to diff.	27.5	4–5	June–mid-Oct.	No	Yes	DNR	No	175

*Hunting is allowed in some areas in the fall (September 15 through November 30); state and national parks do not allow hunting at any time. We would suggest that backpackers contact the district ranger's office for information on specific hunting seasons.

†When complete.

TRAIL	TRAIL DIFFICULTY	TRAIL LENGTH (IN MILES)	TRAIL TIME (IN DAYS)	BEST SEASON	WILDERNESS EXPERIENCE	FEE/PERMIT	GOVERNING AGENCY	CHILDREN UNDER 12	MAP PAGE
19. Isle Royale	Mod. to diff.	170+	5–7	June– Sept.	Yes	Yes	Nat. Pk. Ser.	No	176
20. McCormick	Diff.	—	2–3	May–Oct.	Yes	No	Ott. N.F.	No	177
21. Natural Area	Easy to mod.	13	2–3	Apr.–mid-Oct.	Yes, some	No	DNR	No	178
22. North Country	Mod. to diff.	400+†	—	May–Oct.	Yes	No	Multi	No	179–85
Bessemer	Diff.	12.5	—	May–Oct.	Yes	No	Ott. N.F.	No	180
Bergland	Diff.	30	4–5	May–Oct.	Yes	No	Ott. N.F.	No	181
Victoria to Sturgeon River	Diff.	35	4–5	May–Oct.	Yes	No	Ott. N.F.	No	182
Munising	Mod.	11	1	May–mid-Oct.	No	No	Hia. N.F.	No	183
St. Ignace to Grand Marais	Diff.	135	14–21	June–mid-Oct.	Yes	No	Multi	Yes	184–85
23. Pictured Rocks	Mod. to diff.	42.8	5–6	July–Sept.	Yes	Yes	Nat. Pk. Ser.	No	186
24. Porcupine Mts.	Mod. to diff.	80	7+	June–Sept.	Yes	Yes	DNR	No	187
25. Sylvania	Easy to mod.	30	4+	Apr.–mid-Oct.	Yes	Yes	Ott. N.F.	Yes	188

BACKPACKING IN MICHIGAN

Introduction

When we began looking for nearby backpacking trails, we recognized a need for a guide to help us decide which trails to try. To our surprise we found that there are nearly 1,300 miles of backpacking trails in Michigan and more are under construction.

While exploring the trails, we found evidence of each successive wave of people who have been drawn to Michigan's natural resources. Scenes along the trails included old logging camps, railroads, abandoned mining towns, early settlements with ethnic names, Indian camps and trails, and reforestation following logging and fires.

We bumped into mysteries, such as Who was P. S. Lovejoy, for whom a trailside marker was erected? Or, Who ate all the beans from the large can dump we found, or, What tribe lost the arrowhead we found along the trail? The answers we found enriched the hiking experience. Our exploration also led to fantasies about how Michigan's history might have been different if Europeans had preferred wool hats to beaver felt, if the Indians had discovered gold instead of copper, or if settlers had insisted on stone houses instead of pine.

A hiking trail is never static; it changes as it is used or not used, by season, and following changes made by nature and people. What was once a short hop across a stream becomes a marshy detour following beaver activity. Even this book will bring changes, and for that reason we have included throughout suggestions to help you minimize your impact on the hiking environment. A preliminary word of caution: wherever you hike in Michigan you are walking through history, and without thinking you can easily damage an archaeological site. Everything found should be left as it is, because isolated finds on the ground might indicate a buried site. Never use an old cabin as a source of firewood or take souvenirs from your hike. If you do find some object of interest, take time at the end of your hike to point it out to the ranger.

Future decisions to maintain and construct hiking trails

will be made by government agencies based on the number of people using the trails. We were once puzzled by a blip noise and discovered it to be an electronic hiker counter. We hope this book will encourage more people to backpack in Michigan and encourage those who already hike here to further explore the great natural diversity of the state. The payoff of backpacking is that you learn that you can walk from one part of the country to another. You can carry a load, you learn to keep yourself warm, and you learn that you can survive being a little lost, uncomfortable, or hungry. You may notice a new confidence about life after a backpacking trip.

Equipment

Michigan hiking conditions are different from those in dry areas or in mountains, and so this section will cover those differences as they affect equipment choices. For a more extensive discussion of equipment, you might read *The New Complete Walker* (by Colin Fletcher) or *Walking Softly in the Wilderness* (by John Hart). For some, equipping for backpacking is an end in itself and those individuals discuss at length the merits of each piece of equipment. The goal is to equip yourself so that you can live more or less comfortably along the trail.

Well-chosen equipment will last for many years. If you are purchasing new equipment, you might first consult back issues of *Backpacker* magazine. It is also possible to rent or borrow equipment in order to try it out. Most stores carry only a few of the great variety of tents, backpacks, and sleeping bags available. Send for catalogs from some of the major suppliers listed in the chapter called Information Resources. These catalogs have test and comparison information on equipment. It is peculiar to backpacking that the less something weighs, the more it costs.

Backpacking Equipment

Backpacks. In selecting a pack, take into consideration the high humidity in Michigan. The frame pack, which allows air to circulate between the pack and your back, is the desired choice for summer hiking. If you expect to also use the pack for ski touring, the internal frame or soft pack may be the wiser choice. Stay away from the temptation to buy the largest pack size. Most Michigan hiking can be done with loads of thirty to fifty pounds. Purchase your pack for the type of hiking you expect to do most of the time.

A pack should be loaded to check it for fit. You may find that some packs rub in the wrong places. Certain packs such as the Coleman Peak I and the Hines Snowbridge can be adjusted easily to fit different loads or different people.

Tents. Always! Michigan's climate, insects, and lack of trailside shelters make it necessary to carry a tent. It may sound attractive to sleep under the stars but it would be surprising if you could ignore the buzzing and biting insects enough to sleep. The tent should be lightweight, but not so small that you and your partner will be tempted to give up hiking after two days of rain. The tent should be waterproof or have a rain fly and be equipped with mosquito netting.

High winds are seldom a problem in Michigan and you can almost always find a flat spot and soft ground to set up your tent. The more expensive mountain tents are not necessary here.

Sleeping bags. No bag is going to be ideal for both summer and winter, so you should consider your most frequent type of use. By using the temperature range chart that follows and a knowledge of your own body, you should be able to find a bag that will be comfortable much of the time. Sleeping bags filled with synthetic fibers are bulkier and weigh slightly more than down-filled bags but they retain their warmth when wet, which can be an advantage in Michigan's climate.

For July and August, a bag comfortable to 30° is adequate; for May, June, and September, to 20°; in April and October, to 15°. For cold weather camping you can add an overbag or liner.

Sleeping pads. Three types of sleeping pads are being used for backpacking. Closed-cell pads, such as Ensolite or blue pads, provide excellent insulation and moderate comfort. They are available from short to full lengths. Open-cell foam pads from 1 to 2 inches thick provide excellent summer comfort. Because of their bulk, they are generally shoulder-to-hip length. Newer self-inflating pads are good for summer or winter if you can stay on top of them. The lack of cohesiveness between the sleeping bag and the pad's slippery cover is frustrating. In the long, dark night when you are all cinched into your mummy bag, it is difficult to reposition your pad.

Backpacking stoves. Stoves are required in some Michigan areas at all times and in others when the fire risk is high. The weight of the stove is small, and you will be grateful for the convenience on a cold morning or after you have hiked longer than you intended. The hiker's goal to "leave no trace" can be more easily achieved by using a stove rather than building a fire.

Most hikers use the stoves that burn white gas or camping fuel. Stoves are also available that burn pressurized butane stored in canisters. The butane becomes less efficient in cold weather and some accidents with the canisters have been reported in recent hiking magazines. The canisters pose a disposal problem, and it is not easy to determine how much fuel is left.

It is not unusual to find hikers who have been using their gas Svea or Optimus stoves for ten to fifteen years. The Coleman Peak I stove is another good alternative for backpacking.

Compasses and maps. The most important thing about a compass is the string that attaches it to your buttonhole or beltloop; a misplaced compass is as useless as no compass at all. Ten to twenty dollars will buy a basic compass. Fifty dollars will buy the Cadillac of compasses.

A recent official trail map will usually be adequate for Lower Peninsula hiking. Frequent road and stream crossings act as checkpoints. A U.S. Geological Survey map will add interest but most backpacking trails do not appear on these maps.

The survey maps will be more useful and important in the remote areas of the Upper Peninsula. Reference checkpoints will usually be marshes and streams rather than elevations. An index to the topographic maps of Michigan and an order form can be obtained by writing to the U.S. Geological Survey, Distribution Branch, Denver Federal Center, Denver, Colorado 80225.

First Aid

Whether one is hiking alone or in a group, a first aid kit should be included, and someone should know how to use it. While you are waiting for the hiking season to begin, why not study first aid? Techniques may have changed since you last took the course. Most first aid situations involve discomfort rather than a threat to life. A list of items that might be carried in your kit is found in *Walking Softly in the Wilderness*. One item often overlooked on such lists is water. Keep your canteen full and require each person to carry some water.

Because the elevation changes in Michigan are moderate and most trails are near civilization, persons with certain chronic health problems or handicaps can do some backpacking.

Bees are important to Michigan orchards and agriculture. Many woodland species also attract bees. Wasps, hornets, and bees are a more serious threat to the person in the outdoors than snakes or wild animals. You may not know whether you are highly allergic to insect stings, but a doctor can give you a test and tell you what precautions you should take. For more information, see the section on pest control (p. 22).

Michigan has one poisonous snake, the Massasauga rattlesnake. You are not likely to encounter this snake. They are usually seen in the southern part of the state. The Massasauga belongs to the pit viper family. These snakes have a pit where the poison sac is located, between each eye and the nostril. They have elliptical pupils rather than round and two well-developed fangs that show in the puncture pattern of the teeth. The adults reach 20 to 30 inches. Proceed to the nearest medical facility if bitten by the Massasauga. The latest first aid advice is *not* to use snake bite kits with their devices for incision, suction, and constriction. Rather, seek help at a medical center.

If you are hiking with younger children, a poison antidote kit should be added to the first aid supplies. These kits are available in drugstores and contain charcoal and syrup of ipecac. You never know when a child might decide to try the local mushrooms or camping gas. Prompt, correct action is important.

Clothing

Each item of clothing taken along should be essential, sturdy, and comfortable. You can maintain comfort by adding or removing layers of clothing.

Shirts. A long-sleeved cotton shirt that buttons will be the best basic hiking shirt. This will wick perspiration, protect you from some insects, and can be buttoned or left open for temperature control. A cotton T-shirt underneath and a sweater or windbreaker over it will make up your basic summer combination. A turtleneck shirt feels like a steam bath on a hot day.

Coats. A windbreaker or combination rain jacket and

windbreaker over a warm wool sweater or shirt will be adequate for midsummer. In the spring or the fall, and in the Upper Peninsula or on one of the islands, something warmer such as a down- or synthetic-filled vest should always be taken.

Pants. You may have noticed the photographs of the backpackers with the marvelously tanned legs standing on a rock while gazing off at distant peaks. Shorts are wonderful but seldom comfortable for Michigan hiking. Michigan forests and meadows frequently have a growth of thorny bushes, nettles, and hawthorns, and therefore a pair of snag-resistant pants will offer comfort and protection. If the thorns don't get your bare legs, the mosquitoes or ticks will. Research indicates that mosquitoes are attracted to dark blue, so pants of a light color will theoretically lower your bait rating.

Rainwear. You can count on rain during Michigan's hiking season, and this presents the hiker with a dilemma. While most rainwear keeps rain out, it also keeps in all of the body's perspiration. In hot weather or when walking hard, this leaves the hiker feeling damp and clammy. Hikers sometimes compromise and use the rainwear if the temperature is under 60°, or just get wet if it's a warm day over 60°.

Gore-tex parkas solve most of the "inner-rain" problem, although they are more expensive than other rainwear. The perforations in Gore-tex allow perspiration to evaporate but will not allow larger raindrops through. Underarm zippers are also helpful.

Hypothermia is a *real* emergency. This serious loss of body temperature can occur even when the temperature is well above freezing. Wet clothing and wind greatly increase the danger of hypothermia. Children should be carefully watched, and if they are shivering, they should be warmed up quickly by the removal of wet clothes. A change to dry clothes, the warmth of a sleeping bag, and protection from wind and rain should prevent the advanced stages of hypothermia from developing.

Hats. A knit hat should always be included in your pack. Even a midsummer night can be quite cool and wearing a knit hat reduces the body's loss of heat. If your sleeping bag is not quite warm enough, putting on your knit hat at night can help you get a better night's sleep.

Backpackers seem to express their personality by wearing distinctive hats.

Boots. Most Michigan trails are not rocky and do not require heavy mountain boots. A medium-weight hiking boot or shoe is adequate for most trails. Lug soles cause trail erosion and are not a necessity. Save the tennis shoes for a change when you arrive at your camping site. Your boots should be well broken in and waterproofed against rain and seeping muck.

Michigan's lumberjacks used "lickdob," a hot mixture of tallow, beeswax, and a little lampblack, on their boots. You can probably find a waterproofing mixture for your boots at a camping or shoe store. There is much disagreement among experts on this subject. A survey of hiking friends concurs on the use of an oil preparation once or twice a year to keep the leather soft and a wax preparation such as Snowseal for waterproofing. Experience with sprays or silicone is that they fail immediately wherever the boot bends.

A new innovation in hiking footwear is boots designed of Goretex fabric. They are lightweight and comfortable and many resemble running or walking shoes. There are some cheap imitations of the better boots; we recommend buying a known brand. The down side of these boots is that they have many seams that can leak, as can the fabric when it becomes abraded. They are not as easy to waterproof as all-leather boots.

There are also insulated boots available, but we do not recommend them for general backpacking. As you walk, your feet perspire and the insulated boots become soaked. We suggest wearing a combination of synthetic and wool socks to keep your feet warm and dry. If you are camping in cold weather, you can switch to down booties inside your tent to keep your feet warm.

Socks. Take two pairs to wear, two for a change, and one for a spare. This spare pair can be used as mittens, potholders, or to sleep in. Wool socks provide warmth and keep their shape even when wet. Some combinations or synthetics are adequate as inner socks, but a heavy wool outer sock should be worn for warmth and cushioning. It is a good idea to take your boots and socks off at your lunch stop and check your feet for hot spots or blisters. You can save your hiking trip by applying mole-foam or moleskin patches to these red areas before they become blisters. Do not apply moleskin directly to broken skin or a blister. Instead, clean and dry the area. Then cut a piece of moleskin large enough to surround the area of the blister. Cut out a hole the size of the blister or broken skin and apply. In this way, the pressure is removed from the injured area and it is allowed to remain clean and dry.

Michigan Temperature Averages
(in maximum/minimum degrees Fahrenheit)

City	Apr.	May	June	July	Aug.	Sept.
Alpena	52/29	66/39	76/49	80/53	79/53	69/46
Detroit	56/38	69/48	79/59	84/64	82/63	74/55
Escanaba	47/32	58/42	69/53	76/59	74/57	65/50
Grand Rapids	56/35	68/46	79/56	84/60	82/59	73/51
Houghton Lake	53/31	66/42	75/51	79/53	77/53	68/47
Marquette	47/32	59/41	70/51	76/58	74/58	66/50
Muskegon	54/35	65/44	76/55	81/60	80/59	72/51
Sault Ste. Marie	46/29	60/38	70/47	76/53	74/53	64/46

Source: National Weather Service

Equipment

backpack
stuffbags
water bottle
tent and rain fly
sleeping bag
sleeping pad
backpacking stove
fuel bottle and funnel
pots
pot gripper
cup, spoon, knife, and fork
flashlight and/or candle lantern
50 feet of nylon cord
food supplies
first aid kit
water purification tablets or filter*
moleskin
whistle
repair kit (include needle and thread, spare pack parts, cloth
   repair tape)
bug repellent
notepaper and pencil
compass
watch
maps
personal gear and clothing
matches

Optional Equipment

hiking staff
nature guides
camera
fishing gear
binoculars
thermometer
pedometer
mosquito-net hat

---

*The newest information on *Giardia* indicates that chemical treatment
alone is not sufficient; you must still boil your water for at least two
minutes or use a water filter. See the water purification section for
more details (p. 18).

Backpacking with Ease

Getting Fit and Staying Healthy

Backpacking is a wonderful activity for people of all ages, but there is more to it than simply putting on your boots. Being in good health and physical condition will make your backpacking experience more enjoyable and will prevent injuries. Backpacking has several unique stress factors. They are: the duration of each day's walk, speed and elevation changes, and the amount of pack weight to be lifted and carried. If you will spend some time getting into condition, you will be able to enjoy your surroundings and companions much more. The following suggestions are included to help you get ready.

Our first recommendation is to build up your walking endurance (assuming you have your physician's approval) with a progressive walking schedule. If you are inactive but healthy, start with a short distance—a half mile or a mile three times per week—and over a month's time work up to a distance of three continuous miles.

Keep an honest record of your walks in a pocket or wall calendar. When you are regularly walking at least nine miles a week, add a day pack with some weight inside. Canned goods, books, or water bottles can be used. Increase the frequency to four or five times a week if you need to lose weight.

Put some variety into your walking program on weekends by trying a trail in a local park or in an area with some hills. Take one longer walk before your backpacking trip—at least five miles with a day pack. Walking represents a particularly good, lifelong habit. We have seen the benefits of this on the North Country Trail Association's annual hundred-mile hike. The average age of the participants has been over sixty years of age and some of the older participants are among the first to arrive at the trail end.

National surveys indicate that only 15 percent of Americans exercise enough to get optimal benefits, 45 percent exercise irregularly, and 40 percent do not exercise at all. Additionally, 76 percent of American men and 62 percent of American women—88 million people—exceed their optimum weight as evaluated by the new Metropolitan Life Insurance Weight Standard (which allows thirteen pounds more than the previous standards).* So, when we say that backpacking can be enjoyed by persons of all ages, we realize that 85 percent of us are not exercising enough to be physically fit and most of us are overweight. Be honest and realistic in forming your backpacking plans.

If you are already walking for fitness, you can use this book to find trails to use for a walking vacation. You can replace the sound of cars with the sound of birds or moving water. Here are our suggestions.

Choose a well-marked trail that offers shorter and longer loops. Check our chart and maps. Take along the following: day pack, full canteen, compass, map, snack food, first aid for blisters, and rain gear. Wear layers of clothing to adjust temperature as you warm up or cool down.

Pay attention to map mileage scales. If you know how fast you normally walk, you can use time to know approximately how far along the trail you are. Remember that you will not walk quite as fast on hilly rough trails. If you tend to let your mind wander as you walk your usual neighborhood route, be alert. On the trail you can miss an important trail junction and then your map will not make any sense thereafter.

It is a good idea to drink some water before you start and then sip water about once every fifteen minutes. If you carry your canteen on your belt, it will be easier. Everyone in your group should carry some water. Take a short break once an hour. Stop at the top of a hill rather than at the bottom. It's easier climbing while your muscles are warm. Eat some trail snack food and stretch a little. Look around. A trail walk can open your senses to smells and sounds and can be a wonderful escape from the noise of city streets.

How many miles and how fast you will hike with a backpack depend on such factors as the terrain, the weight you are carrying, your condition, and the speed of the

*From *Aerobics News* 1, no. 8 (December 1986): 2, 4.

slowest person in your group. The weather or getting lost can play a part also. We usually plan to walk for about six hours in a day. If you add rest stops, and lunch, that usually lets you make camp with a little time to relax before fixing the evening meal. If it has been a difficult day, and you are not near a place to camp, you need the endurance to go on. In addition to your physical condition, the other two factors that affect your endurance are nutrition and your water consumption.

Avoiding Injury
The backpack you carry for a weekend or longer can weigh between forty and eighty pounds. You will lift that weight numerous times. Many people bend at the waist, lift, and twist as they swing that weight around onto the back. They are risking back injury. It is better to bend the knees with one leg slightly ahead of the other. Lift with the legs and place the pack on a rock, log, or your own knee. Then put one shoulder through the strap and move the pack around the back. You can also have another person help you by bending at the knees and raising the pack while you slip your arms in.

You can avoid some of the lifting if you have your canteen on your belt and your repellent in your pocket. That way you don't have to put your pack down to get them. It is also possible to take a short rest by just leaning back against a tree. The pressure supports the pack for a short time.

A walking stick provides a helpful third point of balance on slippery trails, logs, rocks, leaves, and hills. A pack changes your body balance, and once you start slipping, it's hard to stop. Just remember that you may be a long way from the nearest road for evacuation. Even a sprained ankle can become a serious problem along the trail. Walking sticks can be plain or fancy. Some people just choose a broken branch found alongside the trail, while others have used an extra ski pole, a cane, or a telescoping pole.

With each step a hiker puts approximately one body-weight of stress, plus the weight of the pack, on the knee, leg, and foot. By comparison, a runner probably absorbs three body-weights of stress with each stride. On a long hike, that is still a substantial workload for the body support system. It just makes sense to lighten the pack where possible, lose a little weight if desirable, and wear boots or shoes with good support.

Tick-Borne Disease

A growing concern to backpackers is a disease known in America as Lyme disease. It was named after the town of Lyme, Connecticut, where it was first identified when a large number of children developed arthritis. It is spread by a small tick that carries the infectious organism. The disease frequently begins with a localized skin rash, starting three to thirty-two days after a tick bite. The rash, which may resemble a bull's-eye, is not the serious part of the disease. Lyme disease is now known to be a complex multisystem disorder. The rash is sometimes followed weeks to months later by cardiac or neurologic abnormalities and weeks to years later by arthritis.

It is important for you to see your doctor immediately if you experience an unexplained skin rash or have found a tick on your skin. Tell your doctor that you have been backpacking and share your concern about Lyme disease. Prompt antibiotic treatment has been shown to prevent or minimize the very serious effects that may show up months or years later.

Lyme disease occurs wherever mice and deer abound. It has appeared in thirty-two states, including Michigan, and every continent except Antarctica. These hard-shelled insects are not fussy and will use deer, mice, dogs, horses, cattle, and humans for the blood meal they need. In Wisconsin, where the disease has been prevalent, there have been losses of valuable dairy cattle.

Lyme disease is not currently a disease reportable to the Centers for Disease Control, so we cannot report the number of cases in Michigan at this time. In the past five years, however, the spread of Lyme disease has made it the most common tick-borne illness in America. No immunity is developed by those who have been infected, so they can be reinfected by subsequent tick bites.

Backpackers need to know several things to protect themselves. Because of the tick's small size, it may escape notice during the forty-eight hours it sometimes takes to satiate itself. Frankly, even in hot weather we advise wearing long pants and a lightweight, long-sleeved shirt. Get in the habit of tucking your pants legs inside the top of your boot socks. Practice mutual grooming with your hiking companions (as chimpanzees or monkeys do). When you stop for the day, examine each other's hair and look over your body for ticks.

Depending on the stage of the tick's life, it can be as small as the zero on a typewriter or up to ¼ inch. If you find a tick, coat it with an alcohol wipe from your first aid kit, some insect repellent, or a drop of stove fuel. This should make the tick let go, without leaving part of the tick in the skin. Then wash the area thoroughly. When you return home, see your doctor and indicate that you have had a tick bite. Not every individual tick carries the disease—but why take a chance?

Nutrition

Carbohydrates, proteins, and fats are the three energy nutrients. High-carbohydrate foods, such as cereals, pastas, grains, beans, and fruits, are excellent sources of energy. They are burned immediately as glucose or stored in the muscles as glycogen for later use.

At the beginning of a hike, the body burns glucose, then the glycogen that is stored in the muscles, and finally, after about thirty minutes, it begins to burn stored body fat along with the glycogen.

Exhaustion occurs when the body has depleted all of its supply of glycogen. The body can replace its store of glycogen each day with a diet that has sufficient carbohydrates. With an inadequate supply, three days of hard backpacking will produce fatigue and reduced speed and endurance.

The best plan is to start the morning with a high-carbohydrate breakfast. This could include cereal, cocoa mix with powdered milk, and some dried fruit. Then munch lightly along the trail. Save the fat and protein meal components for the evening meal. Fats and proteins take a long time to digest, require water and oxygen for digestion, and are best eaten after the heavy physical work of backpacking is finished.

Water

Water is probably the nutritional requirement most neglected by backpackers. It can be hard to obtain along some trails, and it requires time and effort to purify enough drinking water for a group. About 60 percent of our body weight is water and we cannot survive more than a few days without it. Water functions in the body as a solvent in digestion, for elimination of waste, as a major constituent of blood, as a lubricant between joints, and as a coolant for the body.

Sweating is the body's mechanism for getting rid of excess heat. Hot, humid weather can prevent the sweat from evaporating readily, so heat builds up as you are walking. In extremely hot weather wear light clothing, take plenty of water, and hike in the cooler part of the day.

Before beginning the day's hike, consume a cup or two of water and then sip half a cup every fifteen minutes through the hike. This is easy if each person has a full canteen attached to the belt or in a side pack pocket. You should not rely on thirst alone to tell you when to drink. Even when a person has lost three or more quarts of water through hard, physical work, drinking as little as a pint will satisfy the temporary sensation of thirst, but the physical need for additional water remains.

The body also loses water when hiking in cold weather. The body loses moisture to warm the cold air breathed in. We also sweat in cold weather and need to adjust our clothing layers to reduce sweating.

Sweat is very dilute and salt losses are usually insignificant when hiking. Normal food contains sufficient salt and other minerals to replace any salt loss. Sugar-filled drinks slow absorption of water, so plain water is usually best while hiking, although powdered sugared drinks can fill some carbohydrate needs at mealtime.

Water Purification
Michigan is a land of lakes and streams, and yet it is sometimes difficult to find safe drinking water. There are asbestos fibers in Lake Superior, parasites on Isle Royale, and elsewhere a collection of bacteria and viruses.

All forms of water purification are time consuming, and some aren't even effective. The three primary methods are chemical disinfection, boiling, and filtering. The older use of chlorine or Halizone treatment has been found to be ineffective under many conditions and is no longer advised.

You can destroy *most* pathogens by using a form of iodine such as Potable Aqua tablets. This iodine process takes at least thirty minutes to be effective and you may not like the taste of the water. You may be tempted to throw in a package of powdered drink mix. The ascorbic acid in these mixes will interfere with the disinfecting capacity of the tablets and therefore you should add your drink mix only after the water has been adequately treated.

The National Park Service indicates that water should still be boiled for at least two minutes to kill *Giardia lamblia*. They indicate that most commercially available filters do not filter out particles small enough to eliminate *Giardia* or other small organisms. Their recommendation for filtering intestinal bacteria is a water filter with a pore size of 0.4 microns or smaller. According to the brochure from Isle Royal National Park, the two filters that meet that criteria are the Katadyn Pocket Filter and the First Need Portable Drinking Water Purifier.

The cysts of *Giardia* are carried in the feces of wild animals and humans. Following ingestion of *Giardia*-contaminated water, symptoms appear that include diarrhea, gas, loss of appetite, cramps, and bloating. The symptoms may last for up to six weeks and then recur. If you have such symptoms after consuming untreated water, contact your physician. As a rule, giardiasis is not life threatening—just miserable—and can be treated with medication.

Water can be strained or filtered and then boiled for five minutes to disinfect it. This does not mean just heated for five minutes. You should time it after steam is rising from the surface and bubbles are rising from the bottom. If you are going to treat water by boiling, you will need to carry extra fuel to provide each person with enough daily drinking water and water for cooking.

On Isle Royale, chemical treatment is also not adequate to kill the hydatid parasite that is present, and you will have to boil and/or filter all cooking and drinking water except that obtained from water purification systems at Rock Harbor or Windigo.

For shorter trips, you way want to bring extra canteens you have filled at home.

Food for Backpackers

Nourishment is just as important to the hiker as it was to the shanty boys of the logging camps. The cook was usually one of the highest paid employees of the camp. The cook could make or break a camp with the food he served. At some camps, talking was forbidden at the table, thus preventing the men from grumbling about having beans again. You will find yourself eating beans again if you do not give some thought to food for the trail. Books such as *Supermarket Backpacker* (by Harriet Barker) and *The Well-Fed Backpacker* (by June Fleming) will guide you to the alternative possibilities.

In planning your food, keep it simple. The more items you plan for each meal, the more pots you must carry, and the more water and fuel you will consume. You (and your children, if you have them along) will be happier if you are not trying all new foods on the trail. Try some of the foods at home as you prepare for a hiking trip.

Practice with your stove before you go on your trip. They do take getting used to. You may have to find the magic words to get yours to light. If your stove does not have its own pump, a small medicine dropper is invaluable to prime the stove. Fill the dropper with fuel from your tank, close the cap on the stove, put the fuel in the burner cup. Light the fuel and you should soon hear the wonderful roar of your stove's generator. It is a much easier technique than trying to warm a cold stove with cold hands.

See-through Ziploc bags help you organize small food items and find them quickly. We also prefer to put all food items in one stuff sack rather than in miscellaneous pockets. Many backpackers go down the trail discussing how they are going to organize things next time.

Backpacking skillets are a poor compromise. To save weight they are made too small and too thin. Food sticks and burns in the center while the remainder cools quickly. A pan lid can double as a skillet by using a pot gripper for a handle. Leave your skillet at home unless you plan to fish. If you plan to fish, a small skillet with a nonstick surface may be helpful.

When planning your food, give thought to how much water and cooking time each item will require as well as what cooking equipment will be needed. Look at the packaging also, because we sincerely hope you are planning to pack out what you packed in. An extra plastic bag will enable you to store the wrappers until you can dispose of them.

Remember also that there will be days and times when it will not be easy or convenient to cook. It may be raining, the stove may not be functioning, or you may spill your water. Hopefully these won't all happen at once. You will be happier if you know you can reach into your pack for some cheese, nuts, granola, or gorp. These foods are more than snacks; they are a significant part of your daily food plan. For some, they are an adequate lunch. Individuals vary on how much time and money they wish to expend on backpacking meals, as any two people planning a joint hike quickly discover. The following are suggestions that have helped us to keep it simple.

A convenient breakfast is hot granola. Prepackage granola with powdered milk. Put some in a cup and add hot water. There is no pan to clean and it enables you to get a fast morning start—very important when it is cold. Leave the eggs or pancake mix at home or save them for a layover day.

Lunch should not be a big meal; a fruit drink mixed in the canteen and finger foods, such as hard cheese and salami or peanut butter on hard crackers plus raisins and nuts, will suffice. Instant pea soup or a quicly mixed backpacking lunch are other options. Don't stop too long, and save some of your food to eat as you go along the trail.

The evening meal can be a creative one-pot dinner, with a hot drink and a dessert. Instant rice or potatoes take little water and form the base for many supermarket meals.

Foods to Try

Gorp. This is a mixture of some or all of the following: nuts, seeds, M & Ms, butterscotch or chocolate chips, raisins, coconut, and dried fruit. Experiment to find a mixture you like. Put it in plastic bags and carry some in your jacket or pack pocket. It can be eaten while hiking or during short breaks and gives you a pickup when your energy begins to sag.

Pea soup. Many of the instant or dehydrated soups are about as nourishing as salty water. The exception is instant pea soup, which contains filling and nourishing dried peas. You can also add powdered milk to it for more protein.

Spanish rice. Bring water to boil. Add correct amount

of instant rice, bits of salami or bacon bits, dried pepper flakes, onion, and instant tomato soup mix. Cover and let set until rice is soft.

Oriental noodles. These are available in the supermarket in individual packets with seasonings. They require only a small amount of water and three minutes to cook. Add anything you want to them and they become a convenient one-pot meal. You could add a small can of chicken and a packaged sour cream sauce mix.

Instant potatoes. They can form the basis for a filling meal. You can add dried onion flakes, chunks of cheese, powdered milk, or sausage and have a satisfactory dinner. It probably isn't what you would fix at home, but it is quick and cheap.

Hot drinks. Mocha—a mixture of instant cocoa mix and instant coffee—tastes wonderful on a cool morning or evening. Orange breakfast drink mixes can also be consumed hot to chase the shivers. Hot tomato broth is soothing after an exhausting day. It also restores some of the salt lost while hiking. Mix it before you go on your trip. Place in a blender jar the following: instant beef bouillon, instant tomato soup, unflavored gelatin, and a small amount of dried onion flakes. Blend thoroughly and place in a small tightly closed container. To use, place a couple of tablespoons of the mixture in a cup and add hot water.

Experiment with trail foods at home. On a backpacking trip, don't try to eat like you do at home. Some amount of variety may be best sacrificed for ease and convenience on the trail. If your digestive system does get upset while on the trail, give it a complete rest for a few hours or even a whole day.

Pest Control

While the properly equipped hiker will be more comfortable, that is not intended to mean completely comfortable. To go backpacking is to open oneself to surprise and testing. There to test you are ticks, mosquitoes, gnats, flies, bees, wasps, hornets, and other pests. Carry preventive and first aid supplies with you to minimize discomfort from these pests.

Ticks. Wear long pants, a long-sleeved shirt, and tuck

your pant legs inside your socks. Make a habit of looking for ticks on yourself and others. To remove an attached tick, coat it with an alcohol wipe, insect repellent, or a drop of stove fuel. See the section on tick-borne disease (p. 16).

Mosquitoes. Repellents come in spray, foam, stick, and lotion form. Each person should keep some in a handy pocket so it can be reapplied while going down the trail. If you have to stop and wait for someone to dig it out of a pack, the mosquitoes will be having their dessert before you get it on. The stick form has several advantages: you can see just how much you have; it canot spill or leak; you won't be without protection if the container breaks or is punctured; you don't have to apply it with your hands, and therefore you don't have to taste it when you eat some gorp.

Gnats. They buzz around your head and get in your mouth, nose, eyes, and ears. There's not much you can do except walk on down the trail or wear a head net. The swarm usually disappears shortly with a change of sun or wind.

Blackflies and other flies. Keep as much of your body covered as you can. Tuck your pants into your socks. Turn up your collar, put a kerchief over your ears, and keep moving. You may never be bothered by these pests and so you shouldn't hesitate to hike in Michigan.

A net hat that hangs down to your shoulders will keep them out of your mouth, eyes, and ears. These hats can be found in many sporting goods stores. Wearing one is like having a suit of armor. The net weighs little and you do get used to wearing it.

Michigan's clear, fast-running streams attract both people and blackflies. In the Porcupine Mountains Wilderness State Park, Tahquamenon Falls, Pictured Rocks National Lakeshore, and near the Pigeon, Rifle, and Au Sable rivers, you are apt to encounter blackfly swarms from May through July and perhaps sporadically afterward. Even though you are not immediately adjacent to their breeding streams, they may still find you some miles away.

Blackflies do have their good points. The larvae may be a factor in clearing sediment from streams, and they are a food supply for fish. You, the adventuresome hiker, play your role in furnishing the transfusion of blood necessary to enable the female's eggs to mature.

Wasps, hornets, and bees. Don't wear scented deodorants, hairsprays, or perfumes. If a wasp or hornet is buzzing around you, move away slowly; don't flail.

No-see-ums. These are small and cunning. They can come through the netting on most tents. Their bite is bigger than their bark. Repellent is moderately effective.

Furry pests. Yes, Michigan has bears. They are not the nuisance they are in the Smokies or Yellowstone. In fact, you will be lucky to see one. Do haul your food up a tree. If you leave it around your tent you will wake up to hear sniffing and snorting. It will probably be a raccoon family out for a snack, but they can look awfully big in the dark when you are nervous.

Aggressive dogs. A stern *no* may do the trick. If not, remember that a barking dog is probably protecting what he regards as his territory. Circle around the area if possible. Turn your side to the dog; don't directly face him or turn your back on him. If all else fails and he is determined to bite, use your walking stick, boots, or whatever you can to disable him.

Two-legged pests. Recognized by gum wrappers, cigarette filters, cans, and noise. In spite of the fact that you may be on a nonmotorized trail you may encounter dirt bikes or four-wheel-drive vehicles. Both the national and state forest services now have regulations restricting such vehicles to roads or areas that are posted open to vehicles. Neither agency has adequate staff to enforce these rules in all areas. Do stop by the nearest ranger's office to report what you encountered along with the vehicle registration number if you got it while jumping out of the way.

On the Trail

Before you begin your hike, study the map. Notice where the sun is as you start along the trail. Look at your watch and estimate approximately how far you will be in an hour, at lunch, or when you stop for the night. Figure on traveling about two miles per hour. As you hike, check your location periodically at junctions with streams, lakes, or forest roads.

We advise checking your location with map and compass even on well-marked trails for the practice it provides. You can also figure your speed to estimate whether you will make it to your desired camp spot or whether you need to locate an alternate site.

A compass is a magnetic instrument designed to find magnetic North. True North may be a few degrees off. We do not find many maps that give the degrees of correction for true North, but this should not cause you any great problems.

To use the compass, be sure it is level and not affected by a metal object. A nearby metallic object can attract the needle, so you may need to move it away from your belt buckle or other object. Align the North or 360° marking with the needle, then align the North arrow on your map with the compass. The top of the map will not always be North (maps are sometimes turned to better fit on the page). From there, look at the trail map and check your direction. If you are on an east/west trail and should be going south, you may have missed a trail junction. Check your watch to see how far along you should be. Perhaps you haven't reached your junction yet.

In Michigan, unlike mountainous areas, it is usually impossible to pick a prominent landmark and keep it in sight as you move toward it. If you are lost or off the trail and need to hike out to a known boundary, you will need to use your compass to keep a course. For instance, if you know there is a road about a mile north, you can use your compass to find the road. Line up two trees or rocks ahead. Hike to that point and take another compass reading to the north. Pick two more trees or features and hike to them and do it again. If you come to a barrier such as a swamp, use your compass angles to make a right or left correction. Count paces until you are beyond the barrier and then use a compass angle equal to your first correction and hike back the same number of paces to your previous course. You can then continue your previous track north.

It is also possible to use a pile of rocks or brush to mark a spot where you have turned in case you need to return. You might also carry a small roll of surveyor's tape to mark the way in an emergency, for instance, if you had to leave an injured companion to seek help.

Developing a comfortable pace on the trail takes

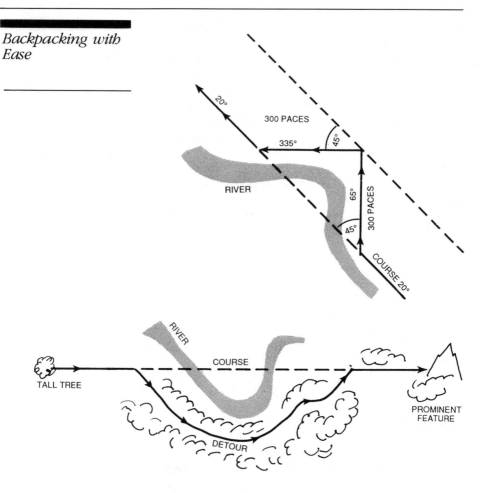

thought if there are two or more hikers of mixed abilities. Keep within sight of the person *behind* you. Change leaders occasionally. Plan a short rest once an hour. If you stop more frequently you do not develop an easy stride and you seem to tire more quickly. On your break, have a drink of water and a small snack; you won't feel as tired and sore if you do this.

At lunch or at a rest stop in early afternoon, check your map to measure your progress along the trail. Try to locate a likely camping spot and decide whether there will be usable water available. If not, look for a spot to fill canteens somewhere along the way.

A grassy opening in the forest usually has a breeze to

keep some of the bugs away and makes a pleasant camping spot. Wind is seldom a problem for the Michigan hiker unless you are on the open shore of one of the Great Lakes. When you have found a pleasant spot, take your pack off and stretch. This is a good time to reach for your soft shoes; take your boots off and let your feet cool down. Take a minute to observe the area before rushing to put up the tent. Don't pitch your tent under a bunch of dead tree branches. If you take a minute to get comfortable, you will do a better job. By this time your body has begun to cool down. You may want to reach for your other shirt.

It's now time for the tent. If you have practiced with it and if you checked to be certain that you have the proper poles and stakes, the only other concern is to avoid setting it in an obvious rain gully. Trenching around the tent is not at all necessary and should not be done because it leaves a long-lasting scar on the environment. After the tent is up, lay your sleeping pad and bag inside. Your bag needs time to fluff up and will feel much nicer after it has been open for a while.

If an outhouse isn't available, select a toilet area at least 100 feet from the trail, camp area, and water. Scrape a small hole with your boot and completely cover with sod and leaves after use. Don't leave white toilet paper flags showing. If you are with more than four people, bring a small shovel for group use. Nature will quickly decompose wastes if some care is taken.

Haul out your food bag and cooking gear. Take stock of your water supply before choosing supper. Allow time to purify water if necessary. Before you begin cooking, give your stove a check to be sure you have enough fuel in it to complete your meal. Cook only as much as you know you can eat. You can nibble snacks later if you are still hungry. That extra uneaten food will only attract varmints to your camp. Cleanup should be done away from lakes and streams. A small combination sponge/scrubber and a drop of soap make quick work of cleanup.

Some prepackaged backpacking foods are enormously salty and spicy, and you may wake up very thirsty in the night. It really helps to have a canteen in the tent for the night. Pack up things to protect them from rain and hang your packs to protect against night visitors. Locate your flashlight. If you have some daylight left you might want to read, play Frisbee, fish, swim, eat again, or explore.

On being lost—no one plans to get lost when starting to explore around the camp area, but because of the thick undergrowth it is very easy to get lost in Michigan woods. It can happen to you, your child, or a companion. Children should be trained to *sit down* when lost. Practice with them. A panicked child can run an incredible distance when trying to find a parent. You could still be nearby. They are probably within calling distance from you, and you will find them. Better yet, they should have a whistle in their pocket. They should blow the whistle three times and listen for a while. Then blow again. Panic is not limited to children. A lost adult will run right past another person and not see them.

If you have wandered away from camp and become lost, it probably is near dark and you feel pretty foolish. Now is the time for you to sit down. Use your whistle or try calling if you are with companions. Listen. Can you hear traffic or a stream? Look. Do you see utility wires, a pine plantation? Check your watch. Time gets distorted when you are lost. Give yourself time to remember where you were on the map, where you camped, and what map features you remember. You should remember that it is possible to survive a night lost in the woods even in winter. Panic is your biggest danger.

After you have calmed down, you can make some decisions. You should always have some survival basics in your pocket: compass, matches, knife, whistle. With these you can make a fire and stay put or use the compass to get out to a road, stream, your camp, or to intersect a trail. However, this isn't the moment to try your compass for the first time.

Off-Trail Hiking

Several new areas in this second edition will appeal to those of you who like exploring off-trail. North Manitou Island, Craig Lake State Park, and the McCormick Tract in the Ottawa National Forest invite this kind of bushwhacking. We advise it only if you are experienced, are physically strong, and are confident in your ability on trails.

Our first suggestion is that you let someone know where you are going and when you expect to return.

Avoid traveling alone. No matter how experienced you are, even a twisted ankle or a severe stomach upset could turn your fun into a serious situation. In these large, remote areas, there are no nearby houses and no passing hikers to assist you. Stay with your companions. If you wander off, they may decide you are lost and spend hours trying to locate you.

Know the area. Take more than one copy of the map. Each person should have a compass. Study the map and memorize its features and boundaries so you could hike out without the map if necessary. We have been in a situation where the only copy of the map fell out of someone's pocket along the trail. Remember this axiom, "a fool and his/her compass are usually parted."

Get into good physical condition before you go. On the trail you can average about two miles per hour. Off-trail hiking is much more demanding. You may progress at only half a mile per hour as you struggle through underbrush, backtrack around swamps, and climb over windfalls.

Extra attention should be paid to your clothing and equipment. Clothes should be snag proof and in good condition. Boots should be able to withstand being wet all day.

The reward of off-trail hiking is the freedom that comes from knowing you can explore anywhere. Relax and enjoy being on the loose. And, as always, be careful and preserve the wilderness of the area.

With Rod and Reel

One of the joys of backpacking in Michigan is the frequent contact with water that is often inhabited by various game fish. Packing along your rod and reel can add a new dimension to your trip and add a new taste to your trail menu.

Michigan offers both cold water fishing (trout, steelhead, salmon, and lake trout) and warm water game fish (bass, bluegill, perch, and pike). The area of your hike and the particular fishing season that is open will determine what you will be fishing for.

You must have a license for fishing in Michigan, and there are a few special regulations pertaining to certain lakes and streams. Licenses and information are available through fishing equipment dealers or through the Michigan Department of Natural Resources, Fisheries Division, Box 30028, Lansing, Michigan 48909. The Department of Natural Resources (DNR) also has a special fishing hotline that has the latest conditions for fishing around the state; the number is (517) 373-0908.

When choosing fishing tackle, remember to keep it light. There are a number of rod and reel combinations that are both lightweight and easy to pack. We use a Diawa Minicast and a rod that breaks down into five pieces. A small assortment of artificial bait should be taken because you may be prohibited from using natural bait or you may not always be able to find natural bait along the way. Artificial worms, spinners, plugs, poppers, and such accessory items as hooks, sinkers, and bobbers can be packed in a small plastic box.

The best times of day for fishing are early morning and early evening. These are also the best times for observing wildlife, so keep your eyes and ears open.

LOWER PENINSULA TRAILS

Lower Peninsula Trails

The trails included in this section are the ones that met our test of providing a good experience for someone carrying a backpack for a weekend or longer. Many local nature trails or short trails in state parks are not included.

We encourage the use of those short trails for day hiking to get in shape or stay in shape for backpacking. They can serve for breaking in boots or trying out your compass. Such short trails can be found in the Shiawasee National Wildlife Refuge, Kellogg Bird Sanctuary, university nature centers and arboretums, and the following southern Michigan state parks: Algonac, Bald Mountain, Brighton, Highland, Hoffmaster, Holly, Ionia, Lakeport, Maybury, Metamora-Hadley, Muskegon, Ortonville, Pontiac Lake, Port Crescent, Proud Lake, Rochester-Utica, Seven Lakes, Sleeper, Sterling, Warren Dunes, Wilderness, and Yankee Springs.

For most of the trails described in this section you are permitted to select your own camping area. The opportunity to set up your own camp seems to meet deep instinctual needs for absolute personal freedom, mobility, and privacy. It is interesting to speculate on the contrast with European hiking, where most hikers stay in huts with large groups of other hikers. Our system will work if each of us practices "no trace" backpacking. Keep in mind that most of Michigan's backpackers live nearest the trails in southern Michigan. You can imagine that they could become "garbage trails" if abused.

The exciting new developments in the Lower Peninsula include work on the North Country National Scenic Trail and the conversion of rails to trails. The first rail conversion is due to be completed in 1988. It is a 23.3-mile, 100-foot-wide track in western Michigan, from Montague in Muskegon County to Hart in Oceana County. Billed as the "thinnest state park," it will be developed as a multiuse trail with a paved 8-foot-wide bike trail and 4-foot-wide hiking and horse trails.

Funds for land acquisition have been approved for a

second such trail from Kalamazoo to South Haven. These are part of a larger statewide plan to acquire abandoned railroad tracks and right-of-ways. Backpackers should work with local organizations and officials to encourage these efforts. As more are developed, they will connect existing parklands, and facilities for camping will be developed. Funding for these trails is coming from the Michigan Natural Resources Trust Fund (state oil royalty money set aside for purchase/development of recreational land).

Allegan State Game Area

Trail distance:	18 miles
Terrain:	level with woods, creeks, and marshes
Trail difficulty:	easy family walking
Best season:	April through mid-October
Governing agency:	DNR
County:	Allegan

Maps on pp. 147–48

This area, with several loop trails, is at its best in the off season. The lovely understory of dogwood is beautiful in May when the white petals sparkle through the woods and in the fall when their brilliant red leaves blend with the sumac and the golden sassafras.

Backcountry camping is permitted from October 1 to April 1. During the summer you must camp at established campsites. These campgrounds take on a circus character during the summer. You may set up your tent and five minutes later a busload of Scouts arrives to set up. They are probably there to do their merit badge hike on the 5-mile Wakazoo Scout Trail.

The trails are well marked and maps are available from the Game Area Headquarters at 4590 118th Ave., Allegan, Michigan 49010. When the office is closed, you can usually find a map in the box on the headquarters porch.

On sunny spring days you may find hognose snakes sunning themselves along the trail. The trails follow streams and marshes, and the hiker may see spring and fall migrations of waterfowl and warblers. Thousands of Canada geese, mallards, and wood ducks may be seen in March and April at the Farm Unit, 3 miles south of Fennville, and also in the Swan Creek marsh. Waterfowl are hunted on a permit basis, as well as wild turkeys, which were first introduced into the area in 1954.

Allegan State Game Area

The area is flat; its sandy soil is covered with oak and pine with a few open areas. Located on the Kalamazoo River and its tributaries, this area serves many recreational activities. Canoers sometimes start below the dam and head for the town of Saugatuck, a summer resort area where the Kalamazoo River joins Lake Michigan. You may want to head there also if you enjoy browsing through art and antique shops. Another nearby stop is the Fenn Valley Winery at Fennville. The winery is open to the public every day.

The trails in the Allegan State Game Area are short and easy. The Swan Creek Foot Trail is suitable for younger children who will enjoy throwing rocks in the stream while they wait for you to catch up. If they become tired, you can easily return to your car.

Beaver Island

Trail distance:	6 miles of marked trails and numerous unpaved forest roads
Terrain:	open dunes, marshes, very few hills
Trail difficulty:	easy
Best season:	April through mid-October
Governing agency:	DNR
Public transit:	ferry or plane
County:	Charlevoix

Map on pp. 149

This island has become a destination for backpackers who want to spend a few days or a week wandering about. The island can be reached from Charlevoix via the Beaver Island Boat Company, 102 Bridge St., Charlevoix, Michigan 49720, (616) 547-2311, from April to December. McPhillips Flying Service, Charlevoix, has daily flights to the island.

The island is 14 miles long and 6 miles wide, so a substantial part of the island can be explored in a week. Hiking is on old lumber and farm roads, across dune areas, and on a few miles of trail. Much of the island is part of the Mackinaw State Forest, and there is one forest service campground located 7 miles south of St. James along the East Side Drive. Please respect private property while on the island.

The forest cover is about one-quarter second and third growth hardwoods, one-half pine and small amounts of cedar, spruce, and balsam. The remainder is in fields, grasses, and beaches. The island was depleted of its virgin pine about 1939.

The island resources are being managed for game and fish protection and there is some commercial logging. There are no current plans for further development of campgrounds or hiking trails. When you come to Beaver Island you enjoy it as it is and hope the mosquitoes aren't too bad. The bugs can be a problem because of the extensive wetlands on the south end of the island.

A letter to the DNR field office at St. James will bring maps and other helpful information about Beaver Island and nearby islands.

Individual backpackers usually head for the township park on the north end of the island or to the fishing site on Barneys Lake following their arrival on the ferry. From there you can head to the west beach area where camping is allowed and the wind blows some of the mosquitoes away.

Depending on time available, you might then go south along the beach or road to Iron Ore Bay. During the summer season when it is open, you could visit the nearby lighthouse. The Charlevoix Public Schools maintain the lighthouse and have constructed 5 to 6 miles of trails between here and the Lake Geneserath area. From here, the backpacker can complete the circle, stopping at the Beaver Island State Forest Campground and back to St. James.

While in St. James, you might want to visit the museum to learn more of the era when Beaver Island had a king, James Strang, who reigned from 1847 to 1856.

A struggle within the Mormon church over who was to be the divine leader developed after the assassination of Joseph Smith. The two principal contenders were Brigham Young and James Strang. Brigham Young took his followers to Utah, while James Strang and his followers went first to Vorhee, Wisconsin. Strang objected to Young's favorable opinion of polygamy. When some of his followers left to go to Utah, Strang had a new vision and decided polygamy was acceptable. All of this time, Strang had two wives, one of whom wore men's clothing and posed as his personal secretary.

Strang looked for a place to move his settlement to escape persecution. He decided on Beaver Island and his followers raised money to purchase sections of the island. On the island, agriculture and furnishing fuel wood to passing ships provided the base for a prosperous, flourishing community. Strang was elected to the state legislature. About this time Strang proclaimed himself King Strang. He was later assassinated by a disgruntled follower, and the Mormon community was forced off the island. The island never again enjoyed the economic prosperity of the Mormon era.

Irish immigrants were the next group to settle on the island, and they gave it the nickname "Emerald Isle." The name Beaver Island comes from the shape of the land— you have to look hard to see it. Interestingly, beaver did not inhabit the island until 1932 when three pairs were transplanted there.

Beaver Island

Green Pine Lake Pathway

Trail distance:	11 miles
Terrain:	rolling with bogs
Trail difficulty:	easy to moderate
Best season:	June through mid-October
Governing agency:	DNR
County:	Clare

Map on p. 150

This 11-mile pathway was developed for skiers, snow-shoers, and hikers. Located in the center of the Lower Peninsula about 14 miles from Clare (off M-115), it is a good option for a weekend hike. You can start at either Pike Lake or Mud Lake campgrounds. This would be good for a family hike or to try new equipment. The frequent road and power line crossings and numbered checkpoints help you know where you are and how far it is to the end. If you don't like crowds, start at Pike Lake (thirty-three campsites) and hike to Mud Lake (eight campsites) and then return the next day.

The trail goes from bog to bog to bog and if you are one of the people who thinks bogs are as pictured in *Winnie the Pooh*—Eeyore's "gloomy place rather boggy and sad"—then we should have a word about bogs.

Bogs begin their lives as small, irregularly shaped lakes. Gradually they are filled in as a sequence of aquatic plants, such as cattails, rushes, lily pads, and duckweed, begin to grow, die, and decay, forming peat. Other plants take root in the peat and then shrubs and trees such as leatherleaf and tamarack, and finally larger trees, take root. There is a gradual formation of concentric circles of different vegetation until the lake is finally filled. Bogs are a very delicate ecosystem found only in northern areas of the United States and contain some unusual car-nivorous plants and delicate orchids.

Use your tree guidebook to identify a tamarack tree; these unusual trees are the only conifers in the region whose needles turn yellow and drop off in the fall. For evening hours you might enjoy fishing for bass, bluegill, and pike.

High Country Pathway

Trail distance:	50+ miles
Terrain:	hilly to flat
Trail difficulty:	moderate; some sections remote and for experienced hikers
Best season:	June through mid-October
Governing agency:	DNR
Public transit:	Greyhound Bus Lines
Counties:	Montmorency, Otsego, Cheboygan, and Presque Isle

Maps on pp. 151–53

The 50-mile-long High Country Pathway is the Lower Peninsula's best opportunity for extended backpacking through a variety of forest zones and with near-wilderness qualities. The hiker will see evidence of recent and past logging sites. Some lakes are marked closed to fishing because of ongoing research projects.

The trail marking and maintenance ranges from poor to excellent. Additional hiker use of this trail might improve the treadway and encourage the state to devote funds to this important trail. A portion of the Shore to Shore Trail passes through this region, and the hiker should consult the map to avoid some confusing trail junctions since blue blazes are used for both trails.

This is remote hiking with no nearby stores to replenish food supplies. If you plan to hike the 50-mile loop, you should be in good hiking shape and will probably want a friend along to help carry the supplies. The lower or southern half of the trail has adequate water supplies at campgrounds and streams (you should treat it), but on the northern stretch water sources will be far between and you will have to carry more with you. With a compass and trail maps, you can find your position if you become temporarily lost.

The High Country Pathway runs through the Mackinaw State Forest. This area was a major center of white pine logging. Approximately 25 million board feet of pine went down the area rivers to Cheboygan around the turn of the century. This state forest represents the largest near-wilderness public lands in the Lower Peninsula.

Elk were introduced to this area, and by 1950 the herd had grown to 4,000 animals. An extensive legal battle was waged between environmentalists and the state over the issuance of oil drilling permits in this area. This conflict between energy needs and wilderness preservation will continue to affect the Pigeon River country because it sits on one of Michigan's productive oil fields. For now, there is still the opportunity for the hiker to observe elk in the early morning or evening in clearings. Signs of elk include their tracks and places high on trees where they have rubbed the velvet off their antlers.

Your companions in some of the remote areas may be fishermen. The Black River is rated to have the highest water quality in Michigan. Ernest Hemingway favored the trout fishing in the area and organized parties of friends to sample "the best fishing in the states" and to hunt bear as well. Fishing ranges from brown and brook trout to steelhead, bluegill, crappie, and tiger muskie.

Nearest public transportation is the Greyhound line between Gaylord and Atlanta. Ask the driver to let you off at Johnson's Crossing. Follow the Michigan Shore to Shore Trail along Tin House Lost Cabin Road and Sawdust Pile Road approximately 5 miles to the pathway. With an auto you could begin at numerous points including the nine state forest campgrounds along the pathway.

Shingle Mill Pathway

Trail distance:	6–11 miles
Terrain:	hills and swamps
Trail difficulty:	moderate
Best season:	April through mid-October
Governing agency:	DNR

If you are not in shape for the 50-mile trail, you might first try the 11-mile Shingle Mill Pathway. Pigeon Bridge State Forest Campground is one of two starting points. The trail begins here as two short scenic loops that go through a mixed forest area and then descends to the Pigeon River, where you start on the longer trails. After an open area, you come to the Forest Headquarters where you can pick up fresh water, have a rest stop, and look at some interpretive exhibits.

As you continue along the trail near Headquarters Road you come to the P. S. Lovejoy monument. You might be mystified, as we were, about who P. S. Lovejoy was and why he is memorialized here. A trained forester, Lovejoy brought the Michigan Department of Conservation into the modern era by instituting resource inventory, fisheries research, forest fire management, and game management.

This monument is just a short distance from the Pigeon River State Forest Campground, the second starting point for the trail. This campground, with nineteen tent sites and twenty-two trailer sites, offers the opportunity for trout fishing. You may find everything from tents to large motor homes, and the hiker may choose to camp on down the trail. A short distance outside the campground you choose between the 6-mile and 10- and 11-mile loops.

On the 6-mile loop you climb a ridge overlooking the river and follow it until the trail turns north toward Ford Lake, crossing Ford Lake Road near the lake. The trail follows an old grade for a while until a second crossing of Ford Lake Road. Some areas are thick with ferns and weeds.

Brace yourself for a long last mile. The Forest Service has constructed bridges and walkways through the cedar and balsam fir swamp, but it is very slow going over roots and mucky areas. The ferns are lovely and the mosquitoes large. When you reach the road, cross the bridge to your left and you are back at the campground.

The 10- and 11-mile loops would be a leisurely two- or three-day hike with overnight stops at the old town site of the village of Cornwall or at Grass Lake.

Clear Lake–Jackson Lake Pathway

Trail distance:	7.7 miles
Terrain:	hills, some wetlands
Trail difficulty:	easy to moderate
Best season:	April through mid-October
Governing agency:	DNR

This is a short two-day hike, with opportunities to fish or swim. The trailhead for High Country Pathway and Clear Lake–Jackson Lake Pathway is located at Clear Lake State Park. Clear Lake State Park is located on M-33 past County Roads 622 and 628 in Montmorency County. Clear Lake State Park has two hundred campsites. With numerous road crossings along this trail and lots of campers in this area, this would not be the choice to get away from civilization. However, for first time backpackers or families with varied interests Clear Lake–Jackson Lake Pathway would be a good choice.

Sinkholes Pathway

Trail distance:	1.5 miles
Terrain:	sinkholes
Trail difficulty:	moderate
Best season:	April through mid-October
Governing agency:	DNR

If camping at either the Shoepac Lake or Tomahawk Lake campgrounds, you may want to take the 1½-mile Sinkholes Pathway for an interesting look at an area where limestone caves collapsed and caused this group of sinks. Along this trail are scars from the 1939 fire. You will see one of the few beneficial aspects of a forest fire. The jack pine cones hold tight to their seeds for as long as twenty years until a fire causes them to open. The result is a quick reseeding of the area with more jack pines.

Another fire in this county occurred in the fall of 1908. A relief train on the Detroit and Mackinac Railroad was sent to Metz to take the settlers and their household effects to places of safety. The cars were loaded, started, and had only proceeded a short distance when a fire, burning large quantities of cedar telegraph poles, fence posts, and ties, which had been piled on both sides, was encountered. The fire had been burning for some time and was a terrific furnace; however, the engineer concluded that he could run his train through the fire to a place of safety beyond and made the attempt. As soon as the engine reached that part of the track where the fire had been the fiercest, the rails spread, since the ties had been burned from under them, and the train dropped to the ground in the midst of the roaring flames and terrific heat. Very few of those in cars escaped, because the heat was so intense that all of the wood in the construction of the cars was quickly consumed. Seventeen people lost their lives in that fire.

Oil royalty funds are being used to add additional public lands to the Pigeon River area. This growth and its Lower Peninsula location will make the High Country Pathway an increasingly attractive destination for the Michigan backpacker looking for a week-long trip within a few hours' drive.

Hoist Lakes Foot Travel Area

Trail distance:	20 miles with shorter loops
Terrain:	rolling with pothole lakes
Trail difficulty:	moderate hiking in remote area
Best season:	all year, except hunting season from September 15 to November 30
Governing agency:	Huron-Manistee National Forest
County:	Alcona

Map on p. 154

The Hoist Lakes Foot Travel Area with some 10,600 acres is becoming known as one of the best destinations on the east side of the Lower Peninsula. Weekend and holiday use of the areas is moderate, but midweek you will see few other hikers. The 20 miles of trails wind their way through pine, aspen, and hardwood. The rolling topography adds interest to this trail; you never know what you will find over the next rise. There are small pothole lakes, marshes, and areas of beaver flooding. The topography has probably contributed to the area not being developed after it was logged—it would not be easy to farm or turn into pine plantations.

With many loops to lengthen or shorten a hike, this would be an excellent area to introduce children or yourself to a wilderness experience. The few old two-track roads through the area have been blocked off to keep the foot travel area free from the sights, sounds, and frantic pace of motorized society. The animals benefit as well, and the area provides habitat for many game and nongame species such as white-tailed deer, black bear, raccoon, red fox, coyote, beaver, otter, mink, badger, and skunk. Porcupines and squirrels are abundant. You may also observe turkey, ruffed grouse, woodcocks, hawks, owls, songbirds, and waterfowl. A few sharptail grouse are also reported in the area.

Fishermen are permitted to carry small boats, canoes, and inflatable rafts in and out of the foot travel area. South Hoist Lake is stocked with rainbow trout; North Hoist Lake offers bass and sunfish, and you can try your luck for perch and bass in Byron Lake. No motors are allowed.

The current management plan includes summer backcountry patrollers who hike the trails to assure that existing rules are followed. These include: no camping or fires within 200 feet of a lake or trail; party size limited to ten people; and pack out what you pack in. There are two wells with hand pumps—one on the west side near Carp Lake and the other at the junction of the trail from the parking area to the east loop trail.

The Reid Lake Foot Travel Area is several miles east of Hoist Lakes and offers a 6-mile trail around Reid Lake through gently rolling land. This would be a good day hike.

This area is now marked with fourteen location posts and trail difficulty markers for skiers. Camping is semi-developed at South Hoist Lake where there are benches and a fire ring. Byron Lake is a jewel with a great sand bottom. Four excellent campsites are on top of the bluff on the north side of the lake. Other camping sites are on the south side of the lake. Follow the unmarked trail around the west end of the lake. All sites have benches and fire rings.

Jordan River Pathway

Trail distance:	18 miles (3-mile scenic loop)
Terrain:	river valley and steep escarpment
Trail difficulty:	moderate; some previous hiking experience advised
Best season:	June through mid-October
Governing agency:	DNR
County:	Antrim

Map on p. 155

To reach the pathway, go 6 miles north of Alba on U.S. 131 and turn west on Dead Man's Hill Road. It is 2 miles to the DNR parking area. You must register at the trailhead. Camping is restricted to the designated rustic camping area, which is 8 miles along the trail. Parties are limited in size to eight, with a two-night maximum stay. A water pump is available at the camping area, but not at the trailhead, so fill your canteens in town.

The trail is well marked with blue paint blazes and blue pathway markers. Blue arrows indicate turns and are helpful where the trail branches off a forest road. The trail begins at the parking area for both the 3-mile scenic loop and the full 18-mile pathway. The North Country National Scenic Trail utilizes the northern half of this trail as one of its links.

This trail is outstanding in beauty; it was the most sensually pleasing of all our hikes. The background buzz of cars disappeared on the first hill, and we could hear water trickling as it merged to form a river. While the adults in our group were enchanted by the wildflowers clinging to bits of rock in the middle of the streams we crossed, the children were equally fascinated with the millions of tent caterpillars seen along the trail. These larvae are gregarious and build a silken tent, usually in a fork of a wild cherry tree, and use the tent as a shelter.

They may completely defoliate a host tree. They hatch in early spring and you will usually see them in May and June.

Your starting point, the Dead Man's Hill section of $7/10$ mile, begins with a long descent into the forest. The surrounding hillside forest contains typical northern hardwoods such as sugar maple, basswood, American beech, white ash, and American elm. The DNR has placed tree identification markers along the trail as well as twenty-five numbered guide posts. As you leave the hillside you enter an aspen timber type made up of aspen, white birch, and red maple.

At various points on the pathway the hiker will encounter the Jordan River. At marker 4 there are interpretive signs that will help the hiker understand the ecology of the 100,000-acre Jordan River watershed. There will be some mucky spots in spring and early summer. The DNR has ditched some of the areas and placed walking logs in others.

At marker 5 you can take the trail left to return to the parking lot or continue to the right on the pathway.

If you continue along the pathway, you will come to the Wild River section of the trail. Here you will see just about every type of fern that grows in Michigan: sensitive, northern maidenhair, Christmas, bracken, ostrich, and common polypody. Active beaver sites exist between markers 5 and 7. You will see a beaver dam, pond, and gnawed trees. The trail crosses the Jordan River at marker 8. The Jordan River became the first Michigan river to be dedicated as a Natural Scenic River and is a favorite with trout fishermen. After you cool your feet, cross the bridge, turn right on the road, and you will reenter the woods about 100 yards up the road.

The Pinney Bridge trail section leads to the campground. The trail follows abandoned logging railroad beds and forest roads, providing easy hiking for the backpacker. As you approach marker 11, you begin another ascent. This climb is worth the effort for the view and the breeze on top. Don't stop to rest too long, the campground is only minutes away.

The Pinney Bridge Hike-In Campground was cleared in 1915 by the East Jordan Lumber Company for their Logging Camp Number 2. The individual sites are widely spaced around the edge of the clearing. A pump provides safe drinking water. Fires are permitted only in the designated fire circles and you must register for your site at the information board. This is a good spot for a game of Frisbee or for some stargazing.

The Cascade Road section begins directly across the road from Pinney Bridge. You will pass through a grassy opening created by the Wildlife Division of the DNR. The very quiet hiker may observe white-tailed deer. You end this section by crossing Cascade Road and enter the Landslide Overlook section.

The source of Landslide Creek is just above the small waterfall. Notice the small log dam that was constructed so the loggers could draw water to ice down the logging skid roads. The trail climbs to a point where the hiker has a view of the western part of the Jordan valley, thus giving this section its name.

The Jordan River Road section crosses Section 13 Creek and an unnamed creek, leading next to the White Spruce section. After crossing the Jordan River Road, you pass through 100 acres of white spruce plantation before crossing the road to the Jordan River Federal Fish Hatchery. The hatchery is ½ mile down the road to the left and visitors are welcome.

When you cross the hatchery road, you begin the Dead Man's Hill return loop. It is 1¹⁄₁₀ miles to the parking area and your car.

Michigan Shore to Shore Riding-Hiking Trail

Trail distance:	219 miles plus northern spur (86 miles) and southern spur (44 miles)
Terrain:	dunes, river valleys, swamps, marshes, plains, and hills
Trail difficulty:	easy to moderate; some remote sections
Best season:	April through mid-October
Governing agency:	DNR and Huron National Forest
Counties:	Leelanau, Benzie, Grand Traverse, Kalkaska, Crawford, Oscoda, Alcona, and Iosco

Map on p. 156

The real attraction of this trail is its length and the opportunity it provides to say you hiked across Michigan. The trail is currently the longest continuous trail in Michigan; it goes from the town of Empire, on the western edge of the state near Traverse City, to Oscoda in the east. The trail can be hiked in sections as well. Frequent road crossings give easy access to the trail.

The trail was developed through the interest and efforts of horse riders. The first section was laid down in 1962, and the first shore to shore trail ride took place in 1964. Large groups make rides in June and September. The hiker might want to avoid those times.

The trail offers easy hiking through a variety of ecosystems. While not a wilderness trail, it is certainly an excellent scenic trail. Some sections of the trail follow the beautiful Boardman and Au Sable rivers. You will have to accept hiking sections along gravel, dirt, or paved roads, as well as forest two-track roads. These two-tracks enable you to walk alongside your hiking companions for conversation.

The most complete trail description is found in *Michigan Trail Rider Association, Inc., Guide Book,* published by the Michigan Trail Riders Association, Inc., 1650 Ormond Rd., Highland, Michigan 48031. A membership in the association includes the guide and periodic newslet-

Michigan Shore to Shore Riding-Hiking Trail

ter updates. The guide is very thorough and usable as an additional hiking guide. Some sections of the Shore to Shore Trail have recently been rerouted to minimize conflicts with motorized vehicles, and so there may be a few sections where your map will be inaccurate. However, the trail is well marked; markers include blue paint blazes, triangular pathway markers, and blue-topped posts with the Shore to Shore Trail symbol of the foot and horseshoe. (On the northern spur, be sure not to be confused by the High Country Pathway blue blazes at those places where the trails cross.)

The trail description that follows is written as if traveling from west to east. You can select your own direction as well as the trail sections that interest you.

Empire to Scheck's Place Camp. Dunes, woods, lakes, and orchards—this section has many scenic overlooks as well as many attractions unrelated to hiking. Near the trail are the Sleeping Bear Dunes National Lakeshore (see p. 77) and the Federal Fish Hatchery near Elmira on the Jordan River. The National Soaring and Hang Gliding Festival is held in early July at Frankfort and the sport is practiced near Empire as well. Few can resist the fruit stands in the area. And there is the Interlochen Center for the Arts at Interlochen offering nightly concerts with major artists, afternoon rehearsals, plays, and art shows. A complete summer concert schedule can be obtained by writing to National Music Camp, Interlochen, Michigan 49643, after May 1. You can even wear your hiking clothes there. The concerts are open-air and, if you smell a bit gamey, it probably won't be noticed as the atmosphere is somewhat informal. Interlochen State Park is across the road.

If you are going to hike across Michigan, you had better get started. The first several miles of trail follow M-72 east from Empire, turning south along Kitlinger Road. Past the airport, you head east across country to Gerry Lake Camp. This camp on state land is 9 miles from Empire, and the hike makes an easy first day on the trail. The rolling hills and views overlooking orchards compensate for the sections that must be hiked following a road. After the day's hike, you can swim in Gerry Lake.

Leaving Gerry Lake Camp, you will have a walk through

hilly woods, meadows, and a view of several lakes. Trails will be on two-tracks, and this section is almost entirely through state land. After the Platte River, your next camp will be Lake Dubonnet Camp—a 19-mile distance. This is the closest trail camp to Interlochen; if you plan a side trip there, you would take Long Lake South Road to Nessen and Nessen to Interlochen—a 4-mile hike.

There is a store in Mayfield where you can replenish supplies before heading on to the lovely Boardman River valley. You may not always find it easy or convenient to stop each night at a campground. You will have to plan your water stops carefully and may have to treat questionable water. The next camping opportunity will be Scheck's Place, a total of 25 miles from Lake Dubonnet. Nearby, Ranch Rudolf offers a canoe livery, motel, restaurant with live music, and campground. Their small store sells some backpacking supplies.

Scheck's Place Camp to Goose Creek Camp.   This section of the trail begins at Scheck's Place State Forest Campground, which has thirty-two campsites and is located along the Boardman River. The Boardman River is a fine river for canoeing and for cold water fishing (trout and salmon).

The trail continues on single- and two-track roads to Rapid River Camp (near Kalkaska) traveling through a mixture of hardwood and softwood forests. After leaving Scheck's Place you will pass near Muncie Lakes Pathway, which is a state pathway for nonmotorized activity (see p. 65). Here, and other places, a double treadway has been marked to give horses and hikers a slight separation. It makes the trail less dusty and we appreciate the effort and time taken. You will encounter a high sand bank after you cross Supply Road. The trail then travels through the Sand Lakes Quiet Area (see p. 75), which is also dedicated to nonmotorized usage. Within the quiet area there is a pathway that visits most of the lakes. Early one morning we observed a number of white-tailed deer feeding near one of the lakes, so keep your eyes open.

The trail follows an old railroad grade from Island Lake to M-72. Once you cross the Little Rapid River you reach the Rapid River Camp. The distance between Scheck's Place and Rapid River Camp is 20 miles. There are toilets, camping facilities, and water available at Rapid River Camp.

After leaving Rapid River Camp you cross U.S. 131 and pass through Kalkaska Swamp, where there is the interesting swamp ecology to observe. After the swamp you follow a number of roads for some 5 miles. Just before you reach the Crawford County line and the Manistee River, you will reenter the woods and soon pass over what used to be a lumber camp. Keep watch for an open area that has the remains of old logging railroad grades. The trail distance for hikers from Rapid River Camp to Goose Creek Camp is 27 miles.

Goose Creek to Luzerne Camp. The next section of the Shore to Shore Trail is dominated by the colorful history of the Au Sable River. The logging industry brought a new era to the Au Sable region at the turn of the century. The river was used to float the logs down to the shore of Lake Huron and lumber mills. Over 1.33 billion feet of logs were floated down the Au Sable from 1867 to 1883. The last log drive on the middle branch of the Au Sable River occurred in 1910, signaling the end of the logging era on the Au Sable.

About the same time that the logging industry was starting, the Au Sable became known also for its excellent fishing and as a vacation spot. The Detroit, Lansing, and Northern Railroad was telling sportsmen to "take your wife and some fishing tackle and go north." The fisherman's delight was the grayling trout, a cold water fish. However, because of the booming logging industry and, some claim, the fisherman's own greed, the grayling was soon to disappear. As the log drives floated down the Au Sable they cleared away much of the undergrowth that shaded the river. This apparently caused the temperature of the river to rise and become too warm for the grayling.

In the 1950s, an attempt was begun to restore the Au Sable to its natural state. The restoration of the Au Sable continues and the river is under consideration for designation as a National Wild and Scenic River. Canoeing along the Au Sable is an increasingly popular activity; and there is talk of limiting the number of canoes permitted on the river daily. Fishing is once again popular with the introduction of brook and brown trout.

Goose Creek Camp is located off County 612 near the Crawford County line. It is operated by the State Forest Division of the DNR and has available twenty-four campsites, toilets, and water. From Goose Creek the trail travels south. Nearby Hartwick Pines State Park might be a good choice for a side trip. There is a logging camp museum dedicated to Michigan's logging industry.

Walking through Hartwick Pines will give the hiker an idea of what Michigan was like before the logging of the mighty stands of white pines. The trail heads south to Grayling where there is a field office of the DNR and a state fish hatchery; both might be interesting side trips also. The trail follows two-tracks into the Huron National Forest and into 4-Mile State Forest Camp. The distance between Goose Creek and 4-Mile Camp is 20 miles.

The trail continues through the Huron National Forest along a number of two-tracks. The trail crosses the South Branch Au Sable River and M-72 then proceeds east into Oscoda County. The trail once again follows many two-tracks and reaches Luzerne Trail Camp, which is provided by the United States Forest Service. The distance between 4-Mile Camp and Luzerne Trail Camp is 21 miles.

Luzerne Trail Camp to Oscoda. The Luzerne Trail Camp is a good access point with camping and parking facilities available. Luzerne Trail Camp can be reached from a side trail that takes the hiker across Durfee Road and then back to the main trail. Mio is a little off the trail, but you could go see the statue of the Kirtland's warbler, restock supplies, and visit the United States Forest Service District Office. There you can ask about the possibility of visiting the special management area for the Kirtland's warbler.

The Kirtland's warbler has its only breeding ground in this area of Michigan. It is a large warbler, approximately six inches in size, blue-gray above and yellow below with black streaks on its wings and back. It builds its nest on the ground and lays four white eggs with brown dots. The bird characteristically wags its tail up and down.

Kirtland's Warbler was discovered by Dr. J. P. Kirtland near Cleveland, Ohio, May 13, 1851. He captured a male bird which was scientifically examined, and credited by both Latin and common names to the discoverer. Just as Columbus did not discover America, so it was found, years after Dr. Kirtland's discovery, that as far back as October, 1841, Dr. Samuel Cabot of Boston captured a male on shipboard near the Bahamas. By 1879 there were but nine known specimens of this bird. To this day it is the rarest of North American Warblers. Its winter home has been found in the Bahamas and there only.*

Besides nesting in a small geographical area, the bird is further limited by inhabiting only the young stands of jack pine from 5 to 18 feet tall. Once the jack pines reach 20 feet, the Kirtland's abandon them. The jack pine cones remain tightly closed for many years or until the heat of a fire causes them to open and release their seed. The jack pine is a short scrubby pine with very short needles (⅝ inch to 1¼ inch) in pairs. The tightly closed cones usually have a slight curve to them. The jack pines grow in sandy or poor soil. Hikers describe the jack pine areas as little Saharas. The United States Forest Service and Michigan DNR are utilizing controlled burning to generate new stands of young jack pine for the Kirtland's and have established a sanctuary to protect this endangered songbird.

It is 24 miles from Luzerne Trail Camp to McKinley Camp, so you will probably have to select your own camping spot for the night. There is a picnic area just after the crossing of M-33 south of Mio. On leaving this picnic spot, you will hike through hardwoods and tall pines. You should be able to find a pleasant camping spot there.

From McKinley Camp the trail will closely follow the Au Sable with many opportunities for fine views of the river. Hikers can camp anywhere within the forests but are reminded to check on fire conditions with the nearest district office of the United States Forest Service in Mio, (517) 826-3717; Harrisville, (517) 724-6471; or East Tawas, (517) 362-4477.

From here, the trail heads south 10 miles to South Branch Camp for horse riders. Backpackers might want to continue 3 miles to the Rollways Camp on Loud Dam Pond. Nearby are a store and two restaurants if you are tired of cooking.

---

*T. Gilbert Pearson, ed., *Birds of America* (Garden City, N.Y.: Doubleday and Co., 1936).

The next campground of interest to backpackers will be the United States Forest Service Monument campground at Monument Road near the Lumberman's Monument. From this area, the trail formerly headed southeast to Tawas. It is still listed by the Trailriders as an alternate route although much of the way is on roads. The trail has now been rerouted to Oscoda to stay within the National Forest lands.

After traveling through some pine plantations, your next established camping area will be at Old Orchard County Park on Foote Dam Pond, one of the impoundments of the AuSable River.

You have just one day to go before reaching the end of the trail. The trail crosses the AuSable River on the U.S. 23 bridge. Follow the signs to Lake Huron. After hiking 219 miles through the forests of Michigan, you can appreciate how important the Great Lakes were to the early European explorers.

The alternate trail will leave the Au Sable. The river continues eastward in a series of dams and ponds until it reaches Sable Point. On your next day's hike to Gordon Creek Camp, you will cross a road nearly every mile. You can then camp at Silver Creek. From here it is just a short hike on roads to Tawas City.

When Gideon Wittemore visited Ottawas Point (later to be called Tawas City) in 1853, the only inhabitants were the lighthouse keeper and two trappers. There was no real settlement on the whole Lake Huron shore between Bay City and Mackinac City.

Wittemore was lured by the promise of a fortune in pinelands and bought 5,300 acres of land at $1.25 per acre. The Wittemore family owned the land, hired the crews, did the logging, hauled the timber, cut the lumber, and arranged for its sale and transportation. They also owned the only store in Tawas City and controlled the government when the county was organized in 1857. This was obviously before antitrust laws. The tenth year of the community was marked by the first session of school, taught by the lighthouse keeper's daughter and held in the Wittemore store. By 1866, lumbering had expanded to the Au Sable River and the settlement at Tawas City had grown to a population of 1,000, very close to what it is today.

Michigan Shore to Shore Riding-Hiking Trail

The alternate trail ends at Tawas City Park. As you stretch out to view Lake Huron's waters and celebrate your arrival at trail's end, gaze across Saginaw Bay toward Grindstone City. Did you ever wonder how all of the lumbermen sharpened their axes? It was probably on a grindstone from Grindstone City. There, huge deposits of sandstone made possible the daily job of ax sharpening.

In addition to the Lake Michigan to Lake Huron trail, the Shore to Shore Trail has a Northern and a Southern spur. They are included here briefly. Because they use roads extensively, we feel that they are of less interest to the backpacker. They could be used as a means of hiking to the main trail.

Northern Spur

Trail distance:	45 miles
Terrain:	wooded, rolling
Trail difficulty:	easy
Best season:	April to mid-October
Governing agency:	DNR
Counties:	Crawford and Otsego

The Northern Spur begins at Goose Creek Camp and 4-Mile Camp. You will head through a stretch of old orchard and jack pine before crossing I-75 on County Road 612. Trailriders use a private campground, Babbitts Camp, about 13 miles from Goose Creek. The trail then heads north into Ostego County.

Hikers on this trail will want to contact the DNR Forestry Office for a list of campgrounds and a map of the Mackinaw and AuSable state forests to plan their trip. For most of this trail you will have to find your own place to camp and treat water. There is one 6-mile roadside stretch along private lands.

The trail in Otsego follows many unimproved roads and two-tracks that wind north to the Elk Hill Campground. There is both a trail campground and a five-site primitive campground. This was formerly the end of the Northern Spur. The trail now continues north another 30 miles toward the planned end at Cheboygan.

There are many streams, floodings, dams, and ridgebacks in the next miles to keep the hiking interesting to the end where Merchant Road joins M-33 in Cheboygan County.

Southern Spur

Trail distance:	44 miles
Terrain:	wooded, some wetlands
Trail difficulty:	easy
Best season:	April to mid-October
Governing agency:	DNR
Counties:	Wexford, Missaukee, Grand Traverse

The Southern Spur of the Shore to Shore Trail begins at the Clam River Trail Camp, located in Wexford County north of Cadillac, east on 34 Mile Road (this might be called Boon or Airport Road on some maps).

The trail travels north from the Clam River Camp along an unimproved road, passing Long Lake. Long Lake has a state forest campground on its northern shore, which is just a short hike west of the trail. Farther north, as the trail crosses M-42, you pass the city of Manton where you can visit a DNR Field Office.

From Manton the trail for the most part follows various roads until you reach Hopkins Creek Camp. Hopkins Creek Camp is located on Hopkins Creek and has campsites, water, and toilets, and is 22 miles down trail from the Clam River Camp.

The trail leaves Hopkins Creek along a gravel road to Lucas Road, which crosses the Manistee River. Canoe liveries are available if the hiker wishes to take a break from walking and wants to canoe the Manistee River.

The trail next enters the Pere Marquette State Forest following many dirt roads and crosses U.S. 131. Just past U.S. 131, you will come to an old Penn Central railway

Michigan Shore to Shore Riding-Hiking Trail

track, which if taken east will bring you near Spring Lake State Forest Campground.

The trail once again follows dirt roads until it dead-ends into the main east-west trail of the Shore to Shore. Turn right and Scheck's Place Camp is just a short hike, and you can make camp for the night. Hopkins Creek Camp to Scheck's Place Camp is a distance of 22 miles and the total length of the Southern Spur is 44 miles.

Muncie Lakes Pathway

Trail distance:	9 miles
Terrain:	rolling forest
Trail difficulty:	easy
Best season:	all year
Governing agency:	DNR
County:	Grand Traverse

Map on p. 157

Muncie Lakes Pathway is located within the Pere Marquette State Forest and is for nonmotorized recreational use. The trail goes to the shores of Muncie Lakes and Dollar Lake, with Island Lake a short distance off the trail. The Boardman River runs along the trail to the south. You might want to pack your fishing gear.

The trailhead is off Brown Bridge Road, and parking is available. Shortly after the hike begins, you will encounter a fork in the trail. Take the trail left to Muncie Lakes, a 2-mile hike. Muncie Lakes are a series of small lakes and marshes; keep your eyes open for wildlife, especially white-tailed deer.

The trail goes north to Dollar Lake and then south to the Boardman River. The hiker might want to combine a weekend of hiking with canoeing on the Boardman River. The Boardman is one of the most scenic rivers in the Lower Peninsula. Canoes and transportation upstream are available from Ranch Rudolf, located off Brown Bridge Road.

The longest loop is 9 miles, with shorter loops of 1½, 3, and 7 miles. The trail is well marked with blue blazes and is an easy trail to hike. Some wet conditions may be encountered near the lakes, depending on the season. The trail crosses dirt roads and would be a good choice for a weekend family outing.

Muncie Lakes Pathway

The forest service has two campgrounds nearby: Fork's Camp with eight campsites and Scheck's Camp with thirty-two campsites. Both campgrounds are located off Brown Bridge Road. Off-trail camping is permitted. We suggest that you do not set up camp right on the shores of any of the lakes. Water if needed can be obtained from the lakes: remember to treat the water before drinking.

Nordhouse Dunes Foot Travel Area

<table>
<tr><td>Trail distance:</td><td>10+ miles</td></tr>
<tr><td>Terrain:</td><td>hilly duneland</td></tr>
<tr><td>Trail difficulty:</td><td>moderate</td></tr>
<tr><td>Best season:</td><td>all year</td></tr>
<tr><td>Governing agency:</td><td>Huron-Manistee National Forest</td></tr>
<tr><td>County:</td><td>Mason</td></tr>
</table>

Map on p. 158

This 4,300-acre area was closed to motorized vehicles in 1976 and is now under wilderness management by the United States Forest Service. It is located just south of the Lake Michigan Recreation Area campground, which is a good starting point for the backpacker because it can supply water. Take time here to visit the lakeside observation platform. The other point of entry is at the end of Nurnberg Road, which runs along the south edge of the area. If this is your choice, fill your water jugs in town.

With only 10 miles of trails, Nordhouse might seem suitable for only a weekend. Not so for the birdwatcher or photographer. What it offers is several luxurious miles of Lake Michigan beach that you might have to yourself. It offers high ridges where hawks keep you company. It offers the opportunity to be delightfully, but not dangerously, lost. Part of the delight is the quiet to hear bird songs and the fresh lake air in which to savor the aroma of wildflowers. On a June hike we identified these birds: Eastern pewee, chipping sparrow, Baltimore oriole, tree swallow, bank swallow, herring gull, purple martin, Caspian tern, prairie warbler, scarlet tanager, chimney swift, cedar waxwing, and great crested flycatcher. And we found just as many wildflowers: devil's paintbrush, golden ragwort, pink twin flower, wood betony, evening primrose, columbine, Solomon's seal, yellow pimpernel, yellow goatsbeard, wood lily, squaw root, yellow hawkweed, Barnaby's thistle, and wild leek.

You should carry a compass and know how to use it. You can camp anywhere in this foot travel area except in the open sand areas along the beach. It is thus possible for this area to accommodate backpackers in the utmost of private camps. It is not an area that should be used by large groups because of the impact such a group would have on the fragile dune areas.

Prior to the road closings, the area was used by dirt bikes and dune buggies and their scars are still visible. The nonmotorized rule is poorly enforced and more Forest Service personnel is needed for aggressive enforcement.

To enjoy this area, hike in and set up camp off the trail in one of the climax growth beech-maple forest areas. Spend the day exploring or on the beach. If you brought guidebooks and camera, you will be pleased with yourself. It may be hard to keep from shooting a whole roll of film on the Lake Michigan sunset.

North Country National Scenic Trail Lower Peninsula Segments

Trail distance:	400 miles when completed
Terrain:	farmland, river valleys, dunes, and lakeshore
Trail difficulty	easy to moderate
Best season:	all year
Governing agencies:	DNR, Huron-Manistee National Forest, Michigan Department of Transportation, some private lands
Counties:	Newaygo, Lake, and Manistee

Maps on pp. 159—62

In March, 1980, President Carter signed the legislation officially designating the North Country Trail as a National Scenic Trail to be coordinated by the National Park Service. When completed, the North Country Trail (NCT) will be the longest national trail (3,200 miles), extending from the Adirondacks in New York State, through Pennsylvania, Ohio, Michigan, Wisconsin, and Minnesota, to Lake Sakakawea in North Dakota. A complete book of maps can be obtained by writing to the North Country Trail Coordinator, National Park Service, Midwest Office, 1709 Jackson St., Omaha, Nebraska 68102. Trails that have already been officially certified as part of the North Country National Scenic Trail bear the official blue and gold marker that symbolizes the points of a compass and the North Star.

Michigan will have the most trail miles, over 800 miles of the total distance. The Lower Peninsula portion starts at the Michigan-Ohio border near Bear Creek, continuing north and west through the Barry State Game Area and Yankee Springs Recreation Area, along the Thornapple, Grand, and Rogue rivers, and into the Manistee National Forest. Near Thompsonville, the trail follows stretches of the Michigan Shore to Shore Riding-Hiking Trail, a section of the Jordan River Pathway, and then heads north to Wilderness State Park and the Straits of Mackinac.

Hiking maps for Michigan segments can be obtained by writing to the National Forest offices, and the DNR at the addresses listed in the Information Resources chapter.

Approximately 100 miles of trail are completed in the Lower Peninsula, while over 250 miles are completed in the Upper Peninsula—much of it across state and federal land. Volunteer groups are needed to work with government agencies to build the trail, particularly in the Lower Peninsula where much of the trail must cross private lands. Most of the North Country Trail is completed in Ohio—even across private lands—because of the presence of the very strong Buckeye Trail Association, which maintains the 1,200-mile Buckeye Trail (the route is utilized by the NCT) around the state. You can help build the trail by joining one of the organizations listed in the Information Resources chapter.

Completed trail segments (1987) in the Lower Peninsula include:

Lake Hudson State Recreation Area	volunteers currently working
Hillsdale/Jonesville Bikeway	5 miles
Barry State Game Area	some existing trails
Yankee Springs Recreation Area	some existing trails
Rogue River State Game Area	7 miles
Manistee National Forest	
White Cloud Ranger District	26.9 miles
Baldwin Ranger District	10 miles
Manistee Ranger District	20.2 miles
Michigan Shore to Shore Trail	35 miles
Jordan River Pathway	9 miles
Wilderness State Park	some existing trails

Only descriptions of the trail segments in the Manistee National Forest are included here. Portions of the Shore to Shore Trail and the Jordan River Pathway are included as independent trails. Other segments are short, under development, or do not currently allow camping along the trail.

White Cloud Segment
Manistee National Forest

Trail distance:	26.9 miles
Terrain:	flat sandy soil with creeks and lakes
Trail difficulty:	easy
Best season:	all year; avoid deer season
Governing agency:	Manistee National Forest
County:	Newaygo

This section of trail has a long history. About twenty years ago, a group of hikers known as the Michigan Trailfinders Club persuaded the United States Forest Service to let them build a hiking trail in the Manistee Forest. It was a case of taking two steps forward and one step back, as conflicts arose with other forest uses, including logging and motorcycling. But they inched along, replacing missing trail markers and clearing a few more miles of trail each summer.

The White River crossing necessitated a swim or a detour for years. Finally, the Forest Service got involved with the trail and agreed to provide a bridge. It took about three years for funds for the bridge to appear in their budget and for the Forest Service to negotiate a land trade with the owner of the best crossing point. The bridge was built in the fall of 1986. A week after it was completed, some of the worst flooding in Michigan's history wiped out large highway bridges all through the area. Hikers rushed to White Cloud to discover the fate of their bridge. It stood. Today it stands as a symbol of the patience of those who were willing to work without quick rewards so that we may now enjoy these 26.9 miles of trail.

When hiking this section you will encounter mixed hardwoods, oak, pine, and poplar forest sections. Logging vehicles and clear-cut areas can disrupt areas although the Forest Service has promised to use buffer zones. The soil is sandy and is easily eroded where off-road vehicles (ORVs) illegally run the trail. There is a patchwork pattern of land ownership, and so to avoid trespassing you should stay on the trail here. If you need to backtrack, there are numerous roads to use.

Exotic and brilliantly colored mushrooms have been encountered along this trail. You may meet local residents with sacks heading for their favorite mushroom-hunting areas. They are curiously reluctant to talk about where they are going. Unless you are really an expert, confine your mushroom activities to taking pictures.

The Loda Lake Wildflower Santuary is a short ½ mile off the trail and is a side trip worth taking. You can eat at the picnic area before picking up your pack again. You can imagine my surprise when hiking on a new trail section near Loda Lake to actually find steps to help me up the sides of a normal roadside ditch. As the U.S. Forest Service has taken official charge of the trail, they have instituted their set of trail specifications designed to keep you from hurting yourself. No longer do you get the thrill of edging across streams on rotten, moss-covered logs.

Camping is permitted anywhere in the forest as long as you are at least 200 feet off the trail or away from a lake or stream. Existing campgrounds are located at Nichols Lake and Benton Lake with additional water at Wayside Park picnic area. Car parking is available at the south end on 40th street, on M-20, and to the north at the Nichols Lake boat launch.

Another side trip is the headquarters of the North Country Trail Association on Felch Avenue. The headquarters is now operated as a hostel facility of the American Youth Hostels. Contact Art or Virginia Wunsch at (616) 689-6876, or write to them in care of the North Country Trail Association, P.O. Box 311, White Cloud, Michigan 49349. The hostel can be used by groups or individuals by advance reservation. It has bunk beds, water, a stove, and a bathroom.

Baldwin Segment
Manistee National Forest

Trail distance:	10 miles
Terrain:	lakes and some hills
Trail difficulty:	moderate
Best season:	April through mid-October
Governing agency:	Manistee National Forest
County:	Lake

The Baldwin Ranger District trail segment is not complete. This might be an incentive for a group to get involved as VIPs, the designation of volunteers in federally managed areas. Contact the Baldwin Ranger District office if you are interested.

Currently, you should park at the Nichols Lake boat landing about 3 miles west of Bitley. The White Cloud section of the North Country Trail joins the Baldwin section here at Nichols Lake. The trail passes near four moderate-sized lakes in the 3 miles to Highbanks Lake Campground. It is only about 6 miles to the end of the completed trail. The continuation of the trail will have to deal with Pere Marquette River and feeder creeks. The U.S. Forest Service has used volunteers and youth conservation corps labor as well as prison labor to build and maintain trails. It never has much money for trail building, although the Eastern Region of the Forest Service has made completion of the North Country Trail a priority and the work is 90 percent finished in the national forests.

To start at the north end, turn off M-37 at the blinker at Star Lake Road (76th St.). Check your odometer. At about 2.2 miles there is a small bridge. Look for the trail about 100 yards past the bridge. It is marked by one of the new flexible signposts with the North Country Trail emblem. These signposts are designed to withstand being driven over by vehicles. They pop back up. We hiked the trail in fall when the bracken fern had been bronzed by an early frost. The trails proceeded along the edge of a former clear-cut area into pines and then a large stand of scrub oak. There was an interesting grass marsh on the left. There are numerous areas to set up camp, but no water supplies until you reach Highbanks Lake Campground in the middle of the trail.

Manistee Segment
Manistee National Forest

Trail distance:	20.2 miles
Terrain:	hilly river escarpment
Trail difficulty:	moderate
Best season:	April through mid-October
Governing agency:	Manistee National Forest
County:	Manistee

There are 20.2 miles of trail completed here. We started in the middle of the trail and hiked the northern 9.1 miles from Coates Highway just west of the boat landing at Red Bridge. You can park at the boat landing. There is an outhouse, but no water pump. Fill your canteens in town.

The trail was surprisingly steep; it even had switchbacks as you worked your way to the top of a hilly ridge line. There were excellent views out over the Manistee River valley. The trail ran through very tall slender maples, with young pines and a sassafras understory. The hilly terrain continues for about 4 miles before leveling off near Hodenpyl Dam Pond.

If you begin at the southwest end of the trail, near Brethren, again a boat landing serves as a parking area. It also parallels the river and includes more wetlands and swamps.

There are two established campgrounds near the trail in this segment of the North Country Trail, one at Tippy Dam and the other at Hodenpyl Dam, but you may prefer to make your own camp on the high ridge above the river valley. You can look out over Manistee Flower Flats and ponder the history of the old Indian boundary marked on the Forest Service maps.

Sand Lakes Quiet Area

Trail distance:	15 miles
Terrain:	hilly
Trail difficulty:	easy; suitable for families with young children
Best season:	all year
Governing agency:	DNR
Counties:	Grand Traverse and Kalkaska

Map on p. 163

Located on the line between Grand Traverse and Kalkaska counties, this 2,800-acre, nonmotorized area was created in 1973 to be a quiet refuge for hiking, skiing, and fishing. This site is suitable for weekend backpacking or to test out new backpacking equipment. If something goes wrong, you are never more than 1½ miles from a road. Families with small children would find this area attractive. It is not suitable for large groups because their impact on the area would be too great.

The area is steeply sculptured, and the sandy trails dip down to the lake levels. There are some confusing fire trails and section line roads, but you should be able to orient yourself with a map and the location of the lakes. Fishing is good in Sand Lake #1 and Big Guernsey Lake for rainbow and brown trout. Your companions in the area may be people who hiked in early in the morning to fish and then leave as you are having breakfast. The Boardman river is just ½ mile south for more fishing.

You may camp anywhere in the area, but you are asked to stay at least 100 feet from the shoreline of lakes. You may have a lake to yourself in midweek and be rewarded as we were by the sight of several deer coming down to the lake edge at dusk. The Shore to Shore Riding-Hiking Trail goes along the south edge of the area, but no horse camping is allowed here.

Sand Lakes Quiet Area

Ugly campfire scars mar the appearance around the lakes. If you must build a fire, keep it small and use an old fire site or carefully lift a piece of sod to cover the fire area after the fire is out and the ground has cooled. Better yet, don't build a fire; use a stove.

Water and toilets are available at the north of Sand Lake #1 or the campground at Guernsey Lakes. Cars can be parked at several places on Island Lake Road and River Road where old forest roads into the area have been closed off.

This area could be more attractive if hikers would bring litter bags and plan to carry out some remains of old can dumps.

Sleeping Bear Dunes National Lakeshore

Trail distance	short scenic loop trails, plus Platte Plains, and North and South Manitou islands
Terrain:	open and forested dunes
Trail difficulty:	easy, great for family
Best season:	all year
Governing agency:	National Park Service
County:	Leelanau

Maps on pp. 164–67

The source of the park's name is the 400-foot-high Sleeping Bear Dune, the subject of a Chippewa legend. According to the legend, long ago a mother bear and her two cubs tried to swim across Lake Michigan from the shores of Wisconsin. Nearing this shore, the exhausted cubs lagged behind. The mother bear climbed to the top of a bluff to watch and wait for her offspring. They never reached her, and today she can still be seen as the "Sleeping Bear," a solitary dune covered with dark trees and shrubs. Her hapless cubs are the Manitou islands that lie a few miles offshore.

Current trails are short and scenic, with the longest mainland trail being 10 miles. Remember that you cannot hike very fast in sand and be warned that steep sand bluffs sometimes collapse. Low tennis shoes will fill quickly with sand and boots will feel hot and heavy. A lightweight boot or high tennis shoe would be the most comfortable option.

When planning your trip to this area you will want to equip yourself for it. Sun and sand are not good for cameras and film. Do not leave your camera in a black case out in the sun. Bring a reflective insulated bag if you plan to do much photography. To keep out sand, store your camera when not in use in a tightly closed plastic bag. The Sleeping Bear area has long attracted photographers and painters, and your efforts should not be ruined by too much sunshine. Also bring along sunglasses, sunscreen, and a hat. The hiking is hot in summer, and you should know what to do for heat-related ills.

If you will stop at Sleeping Bear headquarters, you can obtain maps for the short scenic and informational trails—Windy Moraine, Schauger Hills, Alligator Hills, and Good Harbor Bay. These will acquaint you with the dune environment and serve as a warm-up for the backpacking opportunities of Sleeping Bear: Platte Plains, North Manitou Island, and South Manitou Island. Backcountry camping permits (free) are required for Platte Plains, North Manitou, and South Manitou islands.

Platte Plains Trail

Trail distance:	10 miles
Terrain:	hilly dune area
Trail difficulty:	easy to moderate
Best season:	all year
Governing agency:	National Park Service

This is an excellent trail for families, for a first backpacking trip, or just to enjoy the Lake Michigan shoreline. Stop first at the Platte River Campground to get your free permit from the ranger. She advised us to leave our car in the picnic area parking lot just across from the ranger station. Fill your canteens there also and carry extra water. There isn't a pump at the backcountry camp area.

The trailhead is just a short walk up the campground road. You can hike north to Platte Bay on the bed of an old narrow gauge railroad. It's easy hiking, suitable for tennis shoes. A short trail spur leads out to the beach. To avoid contact with poison ivy, stay on the trail. Poison ivy is a part of the dune plant community and we found it thriving here. Take a break to enjoy the beach here if you are not in a hurry.

The main trail heads east through the woods and a

meadow before arriving at the White Pine backcountry camp area. There are five sites, with a fire circle to be shared by all. In mid-June there were three small groups of backpackers at the site. It was exceedingly clean, including the outhouse.

Another side trail leads out to the beach from the campsite. After setting up camp, we headed over the dune to swim before starting dinner. The beach was deserted except for a colony of geese.

It would be worth staying here an extra night and day hiking the 4-mile Otter Creek loop. Come back for a swim and dinner and then hike out on the third day. On the hike back to your car, you will notice the trail markings change to a black diamond. This is the symbol that makes your heart race if you are a novice cross-country skier. It symbolizes steep hills and sharp turns, and there are indeed a number of those here. The trail dips down along small potholes and swamps giving you an opportunity to see wild irises blooming and to get out your mosquito repellent.

This trail and campground are open in the winter also. You can count on snow cover for much of the winter.

North Manitou Island

Trail distance:	unlimited
Terrain:	flat to hilly duneland
Trail difficulty:	no marked trails; for experienced hikers
Best season:	April through mid-October; limited by ferry service
Governing agency:	National Park Service

This is the larger of the two islands included in Sleeping Bear Dunes National Lakeshore. Like South Manitou Island, it can be reached by ferry service from the town of Leland. North Manitou was acquired by the Park Service in 1984 but final use plans have only recently been completed. Under the management plans, the 15,000 acres outside of the old village area are to be treated as wilderness.

The island environment has been adversely affected by the large deer herd on the island. They were introduced to the island in 1927 and were fed during some winters. Browsing by the large herd has severely damaged the island vegetation, making it more parklike than natural. The deer have no natural predators on the island.

Backpackers can camp anywhere on the island. If you want to camp in the village area, you will need to obtain a permit from the ranger.

One attraction of this island is the remnants of its former life. As you explore, you come across old cemeteries, orchards, logged areas, and remains of homesteads.

The ferry runs to the island on Fridays and Sundays. There are no stores; you're out of luck if you've forgotten anything. Bring enough fuel to boil your water. The island has numerous old roads and two-tracks, but you are invited to explore cross-country on your own.

South Manitou Island

Trail distance:	unlimited
Terrain:	flat to hilly duneland
Trail difficulty:	easy
Best season:	April through mid-October; limited by ferry schedule
Governing agency:	National Park Service

The popular destination at Sleeping Bear for the backpacker is South Manitou Island. Large groups must now make reservations in advance. Memorial Day weekend can be especially crowded. The island is reached by ferry service from Leland, a colorful fishing village. Make reservations early for the ferry by writing or calling the number listed in Information Resources.

The boat ride to the island is about two hours—sometimes much more in rough weather or fog. Take warm clothes and extra food. The boat may not be able to make the crossing and return in rough weather. Advise anyone waiting at home that you may be delayed on your return.

You will be met at the island by a park ranger who will assign you to one of the camping areas, Bay Campground or Weather Station Campground. He will check to be certain that you have a stove, which is required. No pets are allowed on the island.

South Manitou formed during the last glacial age and gradually a mature forest was established. First settled in the 1830s, the island has been successively used by shipping interests, lumbermen, farmers, the Coast Guard, and it now serves recreational interests. Since the establishment of the park, the last of the year-round private owners have departed. What remains is almost a ghost island with an old town, schoolhouse, barns, lighthouse, cemetery, and shipwreck waiting for your discovery.

After you have set up your camp, use your time to day hike to such sites as the shipwreck, lighthouse, and the Valley of the Giants where 500-year-old white cedars are located. The champion is over 17 feet around. The open dunes, wildflowers, and the gull colony offer other diversions. Two gull species, the herring and ring-billed, use this as a nesting area. An overlook trail provides a view of the colony without disturbing their nesting ground. Dune vegetation is fragile, so stay on existing trails in the dune area.

The island is suitable for exploring from three days to a week and for repeat visits. It is a good idea to include a small day pack for carrying compass, lunch, water, rainwear, and guidebooks while you are out exploring. With 12 miles of shoreline, there are numerous opportunities for swimming. The feeling of remoteness has a wonderful mental health bonus for busy people. Rough weather and fog can make it exciting just to find your way back to your tent.

Of the two islands, South Manitou will please the naturalist more even though it is not as big.

Sleeping Bear Dunes National Lakeshore

Waterloo-Pinckney

Trail distance:	46 miles
Terrain:	hills, lakes, wetlands
Trail difficulty:	moderate
Best season:	April through mid-October
Governing agency:	DNR
Counties:	Jackson, Washtenaw, and Livingston

Map on p. 168

This 46-mile hiking trail connects two popular recreation areas in southeastern Michigan. It traverses an area dotted by lakes, including thirteen lakes with easy access from the trail. While camping is permitted only at established campgrounds, there are several rustic campgrounds along the route.

Camping is permitted at Blind Lake, Crooked Lake, and Glenbrook campgrounds within the Pinckney Recreation Area. In the Waterloo Recreation Area, camping is at Portage Lake, Sugarloaf Lake, Horsemans Campground, and Green Lake. Groups can arrange to reserve the frontier cabins at Burns, Mill Lake, and Cedar Lake outdoor centers. A camping permit is required. You can stop at Waterloo State Recreation Area Headquarters, 16345 McClure Rd., Chelsea, Michigan 48169, or Pinckney State Recreation Area Headquarters, 8555 Silverhill, Pinckney, Michigan 48169, for maps and permits.

The Waterloo Recreation Area has been identified as one of the state's best destinations for birds and, therefore, birdwatchers. The woods, fields, hills, lakes, and marshes attract many species. Some of the less common birds that have been seen are sedge wrens, marsh wrens, sandhill cranes, cerulean, hooded, and chestnut-sided warblers, Acadian flycatchers, sora and Virginia rails, Louisiana waterthrushes, and yellow-breasted chats. This

Waterloo-Pinckney

_____

should send you scurrying for your bird book and binoculars.

This is a well-marked trail with numerous road crossings. It offers pleasant hiking for several days. We would advise a 5-day, midweek hike, or go in the spring or fall if you want some solitude. In the summer, plan to enjoy one or more of the beaches. As with other linear trails, you will have to arrange a way back to your car.

Most of the trail has been around for a number of years but the two areas were only recently connected. Over the years, the trail has had assistance from the Michigan Civilian Conservation Corps, the Boy Scouts, the Huron Valley Group of the Sierra Club, and numerous citizen volunteers.

UPPER
PENINSULA
TRAILS

Upper Peninsula Trails

The trails in the Upper Peninsula are remote and rugged, and it is tempting to caution you not to hike alone, to be in good condition, and to be sure your boots are well broken in. In fact, every year groups of city kids venture to Isle Royale in sneakers and manage to have an adventure in spite of, or perhaps because of, some risk and discomfort. The Upper Peninsula offers beauty, challenge, solitude, or companionship. It gives you an incentive to push yourself a little farther.

You will probably be planning a trip of a week or longer when you go to the Upper Peninsula. Fortunately the trails are long ones with many options. Allow extra time for driving on rough roads or possible bad weather. You also need time for dreaming or to allow the images of beauty to be imprinted on your memory.

From Sigurd Olson, who spent many years observing the beauty of the north woods, comes this story.

The Indian woman told me how in the days long before the white man came, a dream net hung in every tepee in the village because mothers wanted their babies to go into the dream world in peace and awaken with quiet eyes.

The net was beautifully made, with the center opening not more than a quarter of an inch in size. I held it out to her and asked the reason for the hole.

She smiled tolerantly and explained it was where the good dreams came through the net; the bad ones, not knowing how, were tangled in the mesh and when the light struck them in the morning, they died.

When I lie in my sleeping bag and listen to the soft moaning of the pines, the lap of the waves, or sounds of night birds in the trees, I often think of the dream net. Sleep comes swiftly then.*

And it probably will come swiftly to you whether you are on Isle Royale, Pictured Rocks, or elsewhere. You will meet something unexpected that will make the adventure uniquely your own.

---

*Sigurd Olson, *Runes of the North* (New York: Alfred A. Knopf, 1963).

Bay de Noc–Grand Island Trail

<table>
<tr><td>Trail distance:</td><td>40 miles</td></tr>
<tr><td>Terrain:</td><td>hills, variety of forest types</td></tr>
<tr><td>Trail difficulty:</td><td>moderate</td></tr>
<tr><td>Best season:</td><td>April through mid-October</td></tr>
<tr><td>Governing agency:</td><td>Hiawatha National Forest</td></tr>
<tr><td>Counties:</td><td>Delta and Alger</td></tr>
</table>

Map on p. 171

The forest service has reconstructed this historic trail that once was used by the Indians and fur traders to travel between the Great Lakes. The Indians for whom the trail and the bay are named were the Noquets; Noquet is generally agreed to mean "bear." Our first knowledge of these Indians comes from the reports made in 1640 by the Jesuit missionary Jean Nicolet, who found them on the shore of Lake Superior. By 1655 they had moved to the bay on Lake Michigan that now bears their name, Little Bay de Noc ("Noc" is a shortened form of "Noquet"). The tribe of Noquets dwindled away from disease and wars. By 1824 there were perhaps fifty of the band remaining at the settlement near the banks of the White-fish River, a short distance from the Little Bay de Noc.

To reach this trail, we traveled west along U.S. 2 and tried to pass by some of the appealing beaches and pasty shops. A word of warning about this staple food of the Cornish miner: don't try to eat more than one at a sitting or that is all you will be able to do—sit.

To begin the trail from the south, take Delta County Road 509 (also called H-05) and go approximately 2 miles north after the turnoff from U.S. 2. Trail parking and beginning are on the left side of the road. The trail begins in a jack pine area and is marked with blue blazes and yellow arrows for turns. About 4 miles along the trail, vegetation changes to poplars and meadows. In the next section you will cross fire breaks, two-tracks, and many areas of lumbering activity.

Just before you reach Haymeadow Creek Camp, you enter stands of birch and beech trees. To reach the camp, take the first two-track past Haymeadow Creek Bridge right to County Road 509 and right again to the campground about 4/10 mile away. The camp has fifteen sites, water, and outhouses. The red, rushing water, club mosses, strawberries, and raspberries make this an attractive stop. It is the only established camp along the trail. You will have to make your own camp for the rest of your hike.

About 5 miles past the camp you enter an impressive stand of red pine and then enter the valley of the White-fish River, which you follow for some distance. A surprise along the trail are the stop signs before road crossings—are they for hikers or horses? Along the east branch of the Whitefish River we saw a doe and fawn. The trail enters a maple-beech forest as it crosses into Alger County. Near the trail junction with County Road 440 is one of the three large assembly areas that have been constructed for horses and hikers. There you will find a parking area, a pump, and pit toilets. These assembly areas are located at the south trailhead, here at the Alger-Delta county line and one on the north side of M-94. At the M-94 parking area, you may continue hiking on a section of the North Country Trail that leads into the outskirts of Munising—thus completing the historic traverse from one of the Great Lakes to another. The trail has now been cleared wide and high enough for horses and riders. You may encounter groups of riders participating in an organized trail ride. This will mean that in places you may find manure, horseflies, and eroded dusty trail sections. It would be ideal to have two parallel treadways where hikers and horse riders share a corridor.

If you arrive at one of the parking areas and find it full of horse trailers, you'll have to decide whether to enjoy the crowd or try another trail to find the solitude you seek.

Bruno's Run

Map on p. 172

Trail distance:	7.25 miles
Terrain:	hills, lakes, rivers
Trail difficulty:	moderate
Best season:	all year; snowshoes in winter
Governing agency:	Hiawatha National Forest
Counties:	Alger and Schoolcraft

There is a lot we liked about this trail in addition to its name. This 7¼-mile loop trail is located in the Hiawatha National Forest 13 miles south of Munising on Forest Highway 13. We arrived in mid-October at Petes Lake Campground to start the trail. The campground was closed for the season already. The trail is a four-season trail, however, and you can camp anywhere along the trail with no permit needed.

In keeping with our interest in outdoor opportunities for persons with handicaps, we were most impressed that Petes Lake has been developed to serve persons in wheelchairs. This would be a wonderful place for a family with a wheelchair-using member to camp. The forty-one-site campground was exceptionally maintained. Each site had plenty of privacy and even included a pole with a hook to hang your lantern on.

In addition to the excellent trail, the area's many lakes can be explored by canoe. There are four carry-in boat access points.

The trail is marked with blue paint and plastic markers. It wanders through maple, birch, and pines, which make a splendid display in fall. The bright evergreen ferns and trailing club mosses provided a striking fall contrast.

The hilliest portion of the trail lies between McKeaver Lake and Forest Highway 2258. Another scenic portion

Bruno's Run

between Widewaters Campground and Moccasin Lake includes an old logging grade and a dense stand of mature hemlock called the Hemlock Cathedral.

We see this as a destination area for a group or family with multiple outdoor interests. Some could stay at the campground to swim or fish while others hiked the trail—either to backpack or with a day pack. Access to drinking water is not a problem here although mosquitoes could be a problem in the early part of the season.

Cedar River Pathway

<table>
<tr><td>Trail distance:</td><td>2- to 7-mile loops</td></tr>
<tr><td>Terrain:</td><td>moderately hilly</td></tr>
<tr><td>Trail difficulty:</td><td>easy to moderate</td></tr>
<tr><td>Best season:</td><td>all year; winter skiing</td></tr>
<tr><td>Governing agency:</td><td>DNR</td></tr>
<tr><td>County:</td><td>Menominee</td></tr>
</table>

Map on p. 173

This pathway is one of the DNR Forestry Division's good loop trails developed for cross-country skiing and hiking. With four loops ranging from 2 to 7 miles, the hiker or fitness walker can make choices along the way. There are nine numbered signposts along the pathway that correspond to numbers on the map. These will be reassuring to a beginning backpacker. These trails also serve families with young children. The shorter loops can even be hiked with toddlers. The Cedar River runs along the west side of the trail and the trail crosses River Road in two places. It would be difficult to get lost here.

It is a pleasant rolling trail through an extensive stand of white birch. It could be used by fitness walkers in the area or for a weekend by beginning backpackers or families with young children. The campsite on the Cedar River has some walk-in sites for hikers and you can also camp elsewhere within the forest. A water pump is located in the campsite.

This area was formerly part of the Menominee State Forest. The DNR has recently reorganized the state forest system into larger units and now this pathway is part of the Escanaba River State Forest.

If you are coming from U.S. 2, go south on County Road 551, which is listed as River Road on some maps. It is 14 miles to the campground road. A small parking

Cedar River Pathway

area for winter use is located just a few feet off River Road. Other similar Upper Peninsula DNR pathways constructed in loops suitable for cross-country skiing and fitness walking include the Cadillac Pathway and the Lost Lake Pathway.

Craig Lake State Park

Map on p. 174

Trail distance:	10 miles, additional off-trail
Terrain:	lakes, rivers, hills
Trail difficulty:	lakeside trail, moderate; remote area for experienced backpackers
Best season:	June-September
Governing agency:	DNR
County:	Baraga

At last, a state park for hikers only and it is a jewel. With 7,623 acres it should please those who want a place to explore and make their own discoveries. It has some marked trails around Craig Lake, but there are many acres to follow game trails or to practice orienteering. We walked in to start the trail around Craig Lake. New signs directed us to a side trail to Sandy Beach campsite. The main trail has orange diamond blazes, with orange circles used for a side trail.

As we hiked along, the term *user-friendly* came to mind. The side trail was well constructed and the campsite had two wood-framed, sand-filled tent pads and an outhouse. Although you can camp anywhere in the park, the use of this site will keep the rest of the park from being degraded by careless backpackers. Don't expect a Lake Michigan style sand beach, however. It is wooded right to the water. There is some sandy bottom here in place of the rocky shore elsewhere. Everywhere we hiked, we scared up partridges. We did encounter a small beaver dam that made us get our boots wet. This would be no problem in the summer but would be a problem in cold weather.

We recommend this area of pristine lakes for a four- or five-day stay. One day you could hike the 7-mile trail around Craig Lake. Another day you could hike over to

Craig Lake State Park

Crooked Lake, or explore the Peshekee River. Swimming, fishing, and bird-watching all promise to be rewarding.

Although this park has been there for a while, we hadn't known about it. You might not find it if you are looking for the usual state park turnoff sign. Craig Lake is administered by the rangers at nearby Van Riper State Park. We advise you to stop by that park office to ask for the latest information on road conditions into the park. There are two roads to the park. We took the shorter road. The turnoff is just west of the turnoff to Nestoria on U.S. 41 and M-28. The road was exceptional—even for the Upper Peninsula. The Park Division recommends four-wheel drive vehicles. We got out periodically to look over the stretch ahead. The road is being used heavily for timber harvesting in the Copper State Forest through which it passes. We don't recommend driving in after dark. It is 5 miles to the Craig Lake State Park parking area. Register at the gate by taking a form to fill out and leave posted by your tent. There is an iron pipe to slip the envelope with your $4.00 per day fee in.

You may carry in canoes or inflatable boats, but no motors are allowed (you wouldn't need them, really). No live bait is permitted for fishing and special size limits are posted. There are several islands one could camp on as well as portages to Clair Lake and Crooked Lake. The park is administered as a quiet area. There are two back-country cabins that can be rented through the Van Riper park office.

Fox River Pathway

Trail distance:	27.5 miles
Terrain:	some hills and wetlands
Trail difficulty:	moderate to difficult
Best season:	June through mid-October
Governing agency:	DNR
County:	Schoolcraft

Map on p. 175

The Fox River Pathway is a 27½-mile trail running between two of the Upper Peninsula's major attractions: near the southern end of the trail is the Seney National Wildlife Refuge and near the northern end is the Pictured Rocks National Lakeshore. Your hike along the Fox River will be enriched by first stopping to see the exhibits and nature trails at the refuge.

As you arrive at the refuge, you may think you hear someone laughing at you. What you are hearing is the vibration of the wings of the diving woodcock. The sound is proclaiming that this territory belongs to the woodcock, and he is available to any females in the area. Other attractions are the numerous geese, and we saw rabbits, weasels, flickers, swallows, purple martins, cedar waxwings, and tiger muskies. The excellent exhibits in the visitor center give information on the types of wildlife and habitat one will find in the north woods.

The trail itself starts 5 miles north of the refuge and is found by traveling north on Fox River Road. You will probably need three or four days to hike this trail and should allow time for getting back to your starting point. There are four small campgrounds along the way: Seney Township, Fox River, Stanley Lake, and Kingston Lake. It would be advisable to carry extra water when hiking between Stanley Lake and Kingston Lake because you will cross the Kingston Plains, which can be hot and dry.

These plains have been set aside as a "stump museum," a memorial to the exceptional pines that once grew here. The State Forest Service has twenty numbered stops along the trail, most of which illustrate some aspect of lumber history or modern forest management. You will hike through jack pine and red pine plantations. You might experiment here to test your perception of temperature. As you hike, guess and then check the temperature differences between jack pine forest, red pine forest, river valley, and open areas. Each will have its own special microclimate. If you are hiking in August, check for blueberries near Stanley Lake dam. The bears won't mind if you take a few. You can also try your luck at fishing for pike in the backwaters of Stanley Lake.

This trail is not well known and you probably won't find it crowded, although you will find people in the campgrounds. If you are still looking for adventure when you arrive at Kingston Lake, you can head north 4 miles on the county road to Pictured Rocks and Twelve Mile Beach.

Isle Royale National Park

Trail distance:	170 miles with numerous loop possibilities
Terrain:	rugged escarpments and ridges
Trail difficulty:	offers a challenge
Best season:	June through September; limited by ferry schedule
Governing agency:	National Park Service
Public transit:	Greyhound Bus Line to Houghton, Michigan; ferry or plane to island
County:	Keweenaw

Map on p. 176

People have been venturing to Isle Royale since at least 4,500 years ago, when the island was the site of prehistoric copper mining. Imagine yourself as part of that small group of Indians.

You travel through the woods to reach the shore of Lake Superior for your yearly stay on the island to extract a small amount of copper for implements. In your group are some of the most able members of the village. The older people stay behind with the children.

You have taken with you the supplies you will need as well as some dried food. Before you can make the treacherous journey to the island, you may have to build a canoe at the lakeshore. In this small, frail, heavily loaded craft you make your way along the Superior shore until you are at a point opposite the island. Then you wait until a very calm day and begin making your way to the island and hope a sudden storm will not arise.

When you arrive at the island, the difficult work begins and it will take all summer. Because members of your village have been coming here for many years, the game on the island is nearly gone. Some of the group will have to spend time fishing.

Others must secure firewood for the mining process. To do this, driftwood fires are set at the base of large trees. By pounding away at the charred wood, a large tree is gradually felled. Then it must be broken into movable-sized pieces and taken to the mining site. The site has been chosen by the green streaks on the rocks.

These rocks are heated with fires and then water is dashed on the rocks to make them crack. By using hammer stones, the rocks are crumbled and pieces of copper are obtained. As the mine trenches deepen from six to ten feet, the debris must be removed. They sometimes fill with water and must be baled out.

As signs of winter approach, the nuggets are loaded into the canoes and you once again make the treacherous crossing to the mainland where the copper will be made into implements and ornaments. These implements are used and traded with Indians as far away as Maryland.*

In more recent years the island has been used for lumbering, mining, commercial fishing, and as a summer resort before becoming a national park in 1940. One visitor during the resort era described it this way:

Washington Harbor is a summer resort for people who have more clothes than they can display at home and who need a quiet place where they can act as a peg upon which to hang their fashionable gowns. The men wear golf clothes, chiefly because of the absence of golf. The women wear white skirts and other absurdities.†

Clothes are still important on the island. Hikers will note the contrast between the newly arrived, clean hikers, their faces glowing with anticipation, and the motley group of people and backpacks strewn haphazardly waiting to return to the mainland.

Preparation for hiking on Isle Royale takes more than the usual thought because it can be cold, wet, buggy, and rough, and you cannot just walk out to the nearest road to escape. Good boots, rainwear, knit hat, and a vest or jacket are important here. You will also want to bring a stove with you because in dry times it is required and in wet times it makes life easier. Check on regulations for carrying liquid fuel on the ferries and sea planes. You may want to purchase that on the island.

The traveling costs, and perhaps the prospect of a long, rough ferry ride, have kept the visitor total low by national park standards—around 15,000 annual visitors. Backpackers will experience occasional full camping areas on either end of the island and some of the campsites

---

*George A. West, "Copper: Its Mining and Use by the Aborigines of the Lake Superior Region," *Bulletin of the Public Museum of the City of Milwaukee* 10, no. 1 (1929): 1–184.
†Charles Dassler and Charles Parker Connoly, "A Memorable Cruise" (n.p.: Isle Royale National History Association, 1962).

along the popular trails. While on the trail, you may not encounter many hikers.

With 170 miles of hiking trails, Isle Royale could be the subject of a book by itself. There are a large number of booklets on various aspects of the island and, for that reason, you will probably want to bring along some extra money, for who can resist such titles as "Fishes of Isle Royale," "Wildflowers of Isle Royale," or "Moose-Wolf Relationships"? Some fifteen publications as well as maps are available at the National Park Headquarters in Houghton or at the Rock Harbor and Windigo Ranger Stations on the island. Look for ferry information in the Information Resources chapter.

When you arrive at the island you will be met by a ranger who will disseminate information about water, permits, gas, and warn you not to get between a cow moose and her calf—as if you would dream of doing such a thing. Any thoughts you might have had in that direction will be quickly dismissed on sighting the island's famous hoofed browser. This member of the order Artiodactyla (even-toed, hoofed mammal) is large. They are ruminants (cud chewers), and feed on aquatic plants, leaves, and twigs, including the island's extensive thimbleberry plants. You will notice these plants when their bristled twigs tug at you as you hike. With a maplelike leaf and white blossoms, you may find you like the berries as well as do the large number of birds and mammals who favor their juicy fruit.

The moose and wolves of Isle Royale maintain a unique relationship. The moose herd of approximately 700 (you will likely see one or more) crossed frozen Lake Superior from Canada during the early 1900s. The wolf pack (rarely seen by hikers) of some 20–40 wolves culls the weak and sick from the moose herd.

Besides the predator-prey relationship, the wolf and moose are joined by the parasite hydatid (*Echinococcus granulosis*) to form an amazing trio. The waterborne eggs of the parasite are ingested by the moose while feeding in the marshes of Isle Royale. The eggs hatch and the larvae begin to mature in the moose's digestive system and move to the lungs where they encyst and reproduce asexually.

When a wolf kills and eats the lung tissue of a moose,

the cyst moves into the wolf's digestive system and matures into a tapeworm. The tapeworm lays eggs that are released into the marshes through the wolf's feces. The cycle is now ready to repeat itself.

Should a backpacker digest the eggs through drinking untreated water, cysts could develop in the lung tissue. If these cysts rupture, they will clog blood vessels and that could prove fatal. It is therefore important to follow closely the rangers' water recommendations. Water should be boiled for at least two minutes or filtered down to 25 microns. Halazone, iodine, and other purification additives have no effect on the parasite. You can fill your water canteens at the tap at the ranger stations but in mid-island you must religiously treat water from lakes and streams. These inland lakes also contain leeches and swimming is not recommended. The cold water of Lake Superior will discourage most hikers from swimming there.

After explaining that Isle Royale is expensive and the water is not drinkable, what is it that brings many people to hike on the island again and again? As you climb the hills and ridges, you get a feeling of wilderness and of the powerful volcanic and glacial forces that have formed and carved this island.

There are numerous named trails on Isle Royale although many are short and serve as connectors to lakeshore campsites. The availability of water taxis makes it possible to start mid-island or to be picked up on the far end of the island and returned to the ferry dock. There are three major trails or loops which would take approximately four hiking days and you should allow for a day of layover or bad weather in a week-long trip.

From either end of the island you can take the 40-mile Greenstone Ridge Trail. You will travel through an area which was extensively burned in 1936 and is now growing back in species that support abundant bird and animal life. Nearly 10 miles of the trail pass through a canopy of sugar maple trees and yellow birch. It is from these woods that Sugar Mountain takes its name. You will climb both Sugar Mountain and Mount Desor, the highest point on the island. The Greenstone Ridge Trail can be hiked the entire way, or you can loop up to the Minong Ridge

Trail or to one of the Lake Superior campgrounds with a dock where you can catch a boat ride.

The most remote trail is the Minong Ridge Trail. This 28-mile trail from McCargoe Cove to Windigo was constructed as a fire trail. It is very rugged and you must make stream crossings without bridges. Water is not available for much of its length, so you should plan carefully. You will see fewer people and might hear a wolf. There are few opportunities to shorten your hike by connecting-loop trails and, because of the numerous bogs and swamps, cross-country hiking is largely impossible.

The Minong Trail section between Little Todd Harbor and the Lake Desor Campground is quite rugged as it follows the glacier-carved Minong Ridge. You will want to allow extra time and drinking water for this section. Again stock up on water for the 8-mile hike to Windigo.

If these longer remote hikes are not what you wish, there are loop possibilities at each end of the island allowing more leisure and visits to historic sites on the island including the sites of prehistoric mining, interpretive trails, and old settlements.

From Windigo you can make a 15- or 31-mile loop. You can go around Feldtmann Lake or take the longer loop via Sugar Mountain and Siskiwit Bay. Along the way you will cross an alder swamp on a 1,200-foot boardwalk.

Isle Royale has two distinct climatic types; it is hot and dry in the higher interior of the island, while the lower periphery of the island is cool and moist. Each climate supports the growth of different forest and plant communities and, along with streams, lakes, bogs, and swamps, gives the island great diversity. This, along with its wilderness quality, will keep the backpackers coming.

McCormick Tract

Trail distance:	unlimited
Terrain:	rock outcrops, lakes
Trail difficulty:	no marked trails; for experienced hikers
Best season:	May to October
Governing agency:	Ottawa National Forest
County:	Marquette

Map on p. 177

If your heart yearns for solitude and you are ready to tackle unmarked trails, no trails, and other adventures, you will love the McCormick Tract and will understand why this was the area selected for the DNR's Moose Lifts.

To find the McCormick tract, take the first road north after crossing the Peshekee River bridge just past the entrance to Van Riper State Park on U.S. 41 (M-28). On some maps this is called Old Huron Grade Road or Peshekee River Road. This isn't a place you will stumble onto unless you are already lost. If you go beyond the paved road, you have gone too far. You should take a road on the right marked Dead End just beyond a direction sign to Arfelin Lake. The McCormick Tract road is gated at the bridge over Baraga Creek. There is a sign and a place to park a couple of cars.

In the closing days of 1987, this site, which straddles the border between Baraga and Marquette counties, was set aside as permanent wilderness within the Ottawa National Forest lands. Environmentalists had struggled for ten years to have the Michigan Wilderness Bill passed in Washington and were successful in setting aside over 90,000 pristine acres statewide.

The full name of this plot is the Cyrus H. McCormick Experimental Forest. As part of the management plan of the area, old camp buildings have been removed. Ottawa

National Forest officials have been waiting for the outcome of the wilderness designation. The area is not expected to change very much. One management question concerns the maintenance of a dam that creates several lakes. The North Country Trail is intended to cross the McCormick Tract. As in other designated wilderness areas, trail signs will be minimal and no facilities will be constructed.

The area receives light use by independent sorts. Usually, backpackers hike in on the road to set up camp at the old building site at White Deer Lake. Then they follow trails over to Lake Margaret, which is the nicest lake. We were personally intrigued by the rock formations that could provide some modest rock scrambling. Use care. We saw no one, including the resident moose, although we did see tracks.

The first twenty-nine adult moose were brought to this area from Canada in 1985. They were joined by another thirty in 1987. The herd now numbers over one hundred and it is hoped there will be at least a thousand by the end of the century. Residents of the area proudly wear moose pins and badges and you will see moose maps posted in local coffee shops. The moose are dispersing into the McCormick Tract and surrounding area. One big bull moose, nicknamed Gulliver, has traveled almost across the entire eastern half of the Upper Peninsula.

The Moose Lift required international cooperation. Team members from both countries assisted with tranquilizing the animals, checking their health, putting them in helicopter slings, and transporting them to the staging area where they were crated and loaded onto trucks. Then they were driven 600 miles nonstop through the night to the release area. All of this was done in the dead of winter.

This is the kind of area that makes you say "ooh" and "ah" as you wander through it. It has enough surprises to fascinate you for several days and then bring you back again.

Natural Area Pathway

<table>
<tr><td>Trail distance:</td><td>13 miles</td></tr>
<tr><td>Terrain:</td><td>sandy ridges and lakes</td></tr>
<tr><td>Trail difficulty:</td><td>easy to moderate</td></tr>
<tr><td>Best season:</td><td>April through mid-October</td></tr>
<tr><td>Governing agency:</td><td>DNR</td></tr>
<tr><td>County:</td><td>Chippewa</td></tr>
</table>

Map on p. 178

The Natural Area Pathway is located in the Tahquamenon Falls State Park, the second largest state park with 36,000 acres. Longfellow's Hiawatha speaks of the Tahquamenon, which translates into "marsh of the blueberries." The Chippewa Indians hunted, fished, and trapped in this area. The pathway travels through the Old Trail Natural Area and Betsy Lake Natural Area. These areas are dedicated to nonmotorized recreation.

The pathway consists of four loops of varying lengths that are all marked with blue blazes. The first loop is called Beginners, a reference intended for skiers. It is 3 miles long and embarks from the Upper Falls of the Tahquamenon River. The falls drop 48 feet, are 200 feet across, and over 50,000 gallons of water cascade down every second. This loop boasts a hike through a beautiful climax forest of majestic beech and hemlock trees.

The 8-mile Wilderness Loop begins the more remote section of the trail and is very typical of the north woods. The forest is generally not heavy, with open spaces, bogs, sandy ridges, and stands of pine and spruce. Along the way you see Wolf Lake, which is a fine example of a bog lake. At the 3-mile mark, foundations are all that remain of a logging camp. Many of the old logging railroad grades are used for sections of the Wilderness Loop. Hikers should carry sufficient water to get them to the area of Betsy Lake.

The Clark Lake Loop is similar in nature to the Wilderness Loop. The trail passes near two shallow lakes, Betsy and Clark, with Betsy Lake having an average depth of only 7 feet. Both lakes often suffer from severe winter kills of fish due to shallow lake depth. The trail following the south shore of Clark Lake is marshy and was recorded as an Indian trail in the 1849 survey. Native Americans visited this area for its natural growth of cranberries. The Clark Lake loop is 5 miles long. The three trails join together to form the Natural Area Pathway for a loop totaling 13 miles.

In addition, the North Country National Scenic Trail follows a portion of the Natural Area Pathway. If you are vacationing in the Tahquamenon area, you could hike portions of that trail as well. You could easily combine some day hikes and an overnight hike in this area.

Tahquamenon Falls State Park has 319 campsites. Modern camping is available at the Lower Falls camp, modern and rustic camping at the Rivermouth campsite. The backpacker is allowed to camp off the trail while hiking the Natural Area Pathway, but registration is required.

North Country National Scenic Trail Upper Peninsula Segments

Trail distance:	over 400 miles when completed
Terrain:	plains, river valleys, forests, rugged hills
Trail difficulty:	moderate to difficult
Best season:	May to October
Governing agency:	DNR, Hiawatha National Forest, Ottawa National Forest, National Park Service
Counties:	Gogebic, Ontonagon, Houghton, Baraga, Marquette, Alger, Schoolcraft, Luce, Chippewa, and Mackinac

Maps on pp. 179–85

Many exciting segments of the North Country National Scenic Trail have now been completed in the Upper Peninsula. Of the 104 miles planned for the Hiawatha National Forest, 78 miles have been completed. Of the 107 miles planned for the Ottawa National Forest, 93 miles have been completed. Additional miles of trail cross state lands such as Tahquamenon Falls, Porcupine Mountains and Muskallonge state parks, state forest lands, and Pictured Rocks National Lakeshore. It is now possible for thru-hikers to cross most of the Upper Peninsula on marked trails. There are changes almost monthly, so we strongly advise you to write to the managing agencies for the latest maps. While exploring trails for this second edition, we were sometimes given hand-drawn maps by the rangers because the printed maps were not yet available.

We have arranged the individual trail descriptions based on two starting points. First, we begin our exploration of the North Country Trail from the western end of the Upper Peninsula in the Ottawa National Forest and work toward Munising. Second, we describe the trail as it begins in the opposite direction at St. Ignace, takes you through Tahquamenon Falls, and ends near Grand Marais. Here you can pick up the trail through Pictured Rocks (see pp. 119–24).

North Country National Scenic Trail

Join us now as we begin our descriptions of the completed trails of the western end of the North Country Trail in the Upper Peninsula.

Bessemer Segment
Ottawa National Forest

Trail distance:	12.5 miles
Terrain:	some steep slopes, waterfalls
Trail difficulty:	for experienced hikers
Best season:	May to October
Governing agency:	Ottawa National Forest
County:	Gogebic

From the western border of the Upper Peninsula, the trail enters the Ottawa National Forest on County Road 513 near the Copper Peak Ski Flying Hill, which is the largest ski jump in the Western Hemisphere. The trail heads north along the Black River to Black River Harbor on Lake Superior. The trail passes near numerous falls along its route: Algonquin, Great Conglomerate, Potawatomi, Sandstone, and Rainbow. Camp overnight at the Black River Harbor campground if you like. You will hike along the road between Sandstone Falls and the entry to Rainbow Falls parking area. It would be a good idea at this point to follow signs into the Black River Harbor Day Use Area to fill up your water bottles. This will be the only source of potable water along this segment of the trail.

At Rainbow Falls there is a suspension bridge with an outstanding view of Lake Superior, a short distance away. You cross the bridge and hike up the bluff to continue along the trail as it heads east. After 6 miles you link up with the Porcupine Mountains South Boundary Road. Hikers can enjoy the numerous trails within Porcupine Mountains State Park, camp, and have a swim or a shower before heading on.

This is high-density bear country. Take precautions. Set up your cooking area some distance from your tent. Hang your food and all trash and garbage from a tree, some distance from your tent. Do not wipe your hands on your clothing while cooking or eating. Avoid using scented personal care products. Make a little noise as you go along the trail. If you do encounter a bear, calmly back away and detour.

Actual recorded black bear attacks are few, perhaps one every five years. That is small comfort to the attacked individual. More numerous are the instances when a savvy bear identifies humans with food and raids a campsite. We have read of cases where people have responded to a charging bear by yelling madly, climbing a tree, or playing dead. Apparently those techniques have at times been successful although we cannot speak from experience.

Bergland Segment
Ottawa National Forest

Trail distance:	30 miles
Terrain:	hilly
Trail difficulty:	for experienced hikers
Best season:	May to October
Governing agency:	Ottawa National Forest
County:	Ontonagon

Look for the trail sign and parking area where the Porcupine Mountains South Boundary Road turns north. The trail heads cross-country following the west branch of the Big Iron River for about 10 miles before angling south. Many of the stream crossings are without bridges.

Look for a narrow or shallow place in the stream or well-placed logs or rocks. Undo your waist strap so you can slip out of your pack easily if you fall. A walking stick planted firmly can help you keep your balance as you cross the stream on slippery logs or rocks. Be especially cautious in spring or after heavy rains. This is a remote area. You will have to find your own camping areas and treat drinking water.

It is also mining country. The Indians were the first to mine the area for copper and they traded it all across the country. Later, European immigrant miners worked the area with pick, shovel, and black powder. You may find old foundations and other historic traces. Please leave them as you find them.

As you continue westward, you encounter scattered escarpments (cliffs) that provide panoramic views across the surrounding north country. You will pass the Bergland Hill Fire Lookout Tower and follow the ridge of the Trap Hills. In this eastern half of the Bergland segment there are four additional parking areas and several road crossings. You can also make a detour to see Cascade Falls. You can end at Norwich road or hike 2 more miles to the end of this completed segment.

Victoria to Sturgeon River
Ottawa National Forest

Trail distance:	35 miles
Terrain:	scenic overlooks
Trail difficulty:	for experienced hikers
Best season:	May to October
Governing agency:	Ottawa National Forest
Counties:	Ontonagon, Houghton, and Baraga

This section begins about 15 miles southeast of the town of Ontonagon. Take M-145 to Rockland, then Victoria Road to Victoria and about 1 mile south to Victoria Dam to find the trail. In late 1987, this section had been marked with blue diamonds, but the trailhead signs were not up yet. You may have to ask or look around a bit.

If it is cold, or the weather is very wet, we recommend an alternate starting point about 15 miles east at Bob Lake Campground off Forest Road 206. In this way, you will avoid the many wet stream crossings in this early part of the trail.

Don't tarry too long here because you are nearing a breathtaking wilderness area. It is about 9 miles to the

Silver Mountain Lookout Tower and scenic view and then you enter the Sturgeon River Gorge area. This is one of the ten national forest areas in Michigan included in the 92,000-acre Michigan Wilderness Bill passed by Congress in the last days of 1987.

The Sturgeon River gorge is the largest and deepest in the Great Lakes states. The slopes climb sharply from the stream to over 400 feet. The river itself has numerous rapids, waterfalls, and oxbows.

The trail is on the east side of Forest Roads 191 and 193, but may later be moved to take advantage of the scenery along the Sturgeon River. The topography ranges from sandy pine plains to a network of ridges. A side trail leads along the edge of the gorge. Take time to see what environmentalists fought for ten years to preserve.

There are two established campgrounds here near the end of this section of the trail. One is the national forest campground on Forest Road 191 at the Sturgeon River. The other is Big Lake state forest campground, 5 miles east on Plains Road.

Special note for NCT thru-hikers. You will need county or USGS maps to continue on eastward. Until you are near Munising, you will not have any more completed marked trail sections, although you will pass two excellent areas for exploration along the way: Craig Lake State Park and the McCormick Tract of the Ottawa National Forest.

From the end of the trail at Sturgeon River, you could walk down to Watton and hike the abandoned Soo Line tracks to Nestoria (approximately 26 miles). Kings Lake State Forest Campground is midway between Watton and Nestoria. If you need supplies, stock up in one of the towns. From Nestoria, you can hike into Craig Lake State Park. See the separate description of this state park (p. 95). There are numerous old forest two-tracks between Craig Lake and the McCormick Tract. It's only 6 to 8 miles between the areas.

**Munising Segment
Hiawatha National Forest**

Trail length:	11 miles
Terrain:	hilly
Trail difficulty:	moderate
Best season:	May through mid-October
Governing agency:	Hiawatha National Forest
County:	Alger

A recently constructed 11-mile segment of the North Country Trail joins the Munising area to the Bay De Noc Trail. About 3 miles west of Munising on M-94, the trail begins. Perhaps a better place to start is the ski warming hut parking area at the second place the trail crosses M-94, 6 miles west of Munising. There are also a water pump and an outhouse located here.

The forest service has used high standards in building and marking this trail segment. The first 50 feet are graveled to avoid erosion. The trailheads are marked with the blue and gold North Country Trail emblem and distance markers appear along the way. The forest service has cleared a narrow path rather than use existing two-tracks in the area. It gives the hiker a feeling of intimacy and privacy along the trail. This area is deeply sculptured and wooded with some overlook areas. It has the constantly changing view that makes a trail interesting rather than boring.

From the ski hut, cross M-94 to the west. You climb a high ridge of hardwoods before dropping into pines. After about 1½ miles you come to an open area before arriving at the ponds. We stopped for a long time at the ponds, watching the bird life and the leaves falling. This is one of those rare places where you hear no traffic, see no people, and can pause and reflect before going on. The trail curves north, before dropping south along Bay Creek to join the Bay de Noc Trail at M-94.

We think that long-distance North Country Trail hikers will appreciate this segment. If you arrive in August and

Pictured Rocks is crowded, this might be a good alternative.

St. Ignace to Grand Marais

Trail distance:	135 miles
Terrain:	rivers, flats, forests, marshes, Great Lakes shoreline
Trail difficulty:	difficult; for experienced hikers
Best season:	June to mid-October
Governing agency:	DNR, Hiawatha National Forest, National Park Service
Counties:	Mackinac, Chippewa, Luce, and Schoolcraft

St. Ignace to Tahquamenon.   In St. Ignace you will want to stop in at the Hiawatha National Forest Ranger Office on Ferry Street to inform them of your hiking plans and get an up-to-date report on the trail. When we stopped in we learned of a trail section that was being rerouted. At the time we first hiked the trail, the St. Ignace District had been marked and cleared but the northern section (Sault St. Marie District) had only been marked. The St. Ignace District marking is a royal blue paint blaze. Some sections in Sault St. Marie are also marked with white diamonds.

Get off I-75 at exit 348, which is the Castle Rock Road exit. Go west to County Road 3104 (Castle Rock Road) and turn left. The beginning of the trail is near the road. The trail heads west across the Soo Line tracks and continues west to Brevoort Lake Campground. This campground with sixty-nine camp units, water, swimming, and fishing would also be a good starting point for the trail.

The trail heads north, crossing County Road 520, and then east across the Carp River. There are numerous bridges that the Forest Service has constructed between here and the North Branch of the Carp River. You will be rewarded, because the next 6 miles pass through a high maple forest area with lush trillium understory.

During a conversation with a ranger we learned that a section of the North Country Trail near here had been relocated because it ran through the habitat of the rare hart's-tongue fern. Ferns are among the least known plants for many of us, who can recognize and name perhaps the bracken and maidenhair types.

The rare hart's-tongue fern was once thought to grow in only two counties in New York State. In a charming 1800s-style book, Frances Theodora Parsons describes her pursuit of this rare fern.

> Guided by the explicit direction of Mr. J. H. TenEyck Burr, a fern enthusiast who is always ready to share with others, of whose good faith he is assured, his enjoyment of the hiding-places of his favorites, we found at last the Hart's Tongue in its own home. . . .
>
> Nearly always it is caught beneath moss-grown fragments of the fallen limestone, the bright-green undulating, glossy leaves either standing almost erect . . . or else falling over toward the slope of the land so as to present a nearly prostrate appearance. At times these fronds are very numerous, as many as fifty to a plant, forming great clumps of foliage. Again we find a plant with only half a dozen or even fewer fronds. At maturity the linear, bright-brown fruit dots, a row on either side of the mid-rib, are conspicuous on the lower surfaces of the fronds.*

Plants such as the hart's-tongue fern have a very specific and limited habitat. Hikers must recognize that they are a part of the pressure causing the disappearance of plant and animal species. As this North Country Trail is developed, care should be taken to route it through scenic areas, but also to avoid delicate habitats.

Continuing northward, you cross into the Sault Ste. Marie Ranger District. Just to the east of the crossing of H-40 is the Trout Brook Pond picnic area. This would be a good break for fishing or lunch. The trail near here is in a red pine plantation with some timber cutting in the trail area.

As you leave the picnic area, you cross the Soo Line tracks again and then have three more creek crossings: Biscuit, Pine, and Hemlock. At the intersection of Forest Road 3132 you enter a clear-cut area and then a cedar forest. The trail then continues north through jack pine and poplars, and you will encounter white diamond trail markers. You are on your way to Soldier Lake Camp-

---

*Frances Theodora Parsons, *How to Know the Ferns,* 2d ed. (1899; reprint ed., New York: Dover, n.d.).

ground, which has fifty-five units, swimming, fishing, and water.

Leaving Soldier Lake you cross M-28 and the Soo Line again. Continue north through a maple-beech forest. No Vehicle signs appear at road crossings. Soon you will see water—it's no mirage but rather Lake Superior. Follow Forest Highway 42 and cross the Tahquamenon River on M-123. You have a choice of camping here at Rivermouth Camp or continuing on the trail past the Hiawatha Club to the Lower Falls Campground.

This hike of approximately 65 miles from St. Ignace to Tahquamenon is for sturdy, unflappable hikers who don't mind some uncertainty. It would be sensible to have with you both a survey map of the area and a county map so that if the flagged trees in the Sault Ste. Marie Ranger District have been clear-cut, you can find your way to pick up the trail. Good luck.

Tahquamenon to Grand Marais.   From the Lower Falls Campground, cross M-123 and follow Clark Lake Road for a mile to the beginning of the Natural Area Pathway (see pp. 107–8). Take a right and follow the northern section of the Natural Area Pathway, which is combined here with the North Country Trail. You will pass Clark Lake and Betsy Lake on an excellent, well-marked trail. The Betsy Lake marsh contains berry bushes, and you will find the foundation of an old logging camp nearby.

A wooden trail sign marks the crossing at County Road 500. You are now in the Lake Superior State Forest and heading north. The trail passes near Pike Lake, which has a campground and can be reached on County Road 414.

The trail runs through the Two Hearted River watershed and then through an extensive open sand plains and clear-cut area. After about 10 miles, it is a relief as you again near the Lake Superior shore. Continue 13 miles on to Muskallonge Lake where there is a state park. The trail in this area is cleared and well marked with blue blazes. There is a good campground, and the rangers are helpful and seem enthusiastic about the trail. Your hike could terminate here or continue on to Grand Marais and the Pictured Rocks.

Between Muskallonge and Grand Marais (approximately 18 miles), the trail follows the lake shore for a

North Country National Scenic Trail

full hiking day before heading inland near the Sucker River. It then follows County Road 700 to Grand Marais where you can stay in a motel if you are trail weary. If not, stock up on food and continue on to Pictured Rocks. The trail through Pictured Rocks is to be a continuation of the North Country Trail but since it is frequently a separate destination, we have described that trail in its own section (see pp. 119–24).

Pictured Rocks National Lakeshore

Trail distance:	42.8 miles
Terrain:	rugged cliffs and sand dunes
Trail difficulty:	moderate to difficult depending upon weather
Best season:	July through September
Governing agency:	National Park Service
County:	Alger

Map on p. 186

Prior to 1840, the white man's impact in this coastal region of the Upper Peninsula was restricted to fur trapping and trading with the Indians. The first settlement of Europeans began on Grand Island in the year 1840. Ten years later, a Philadelphia company began the construction of a resort on the site of present-day Munising. However, the overland trip from Bay de Noc to Munising proved to be too rough for most people. The resort soon failed and closed for lack of customers.

During the late 1800s, lumbering and the railroad came to this area. The Cleveland-Cliffs Iron Company bought some 300,000 acres in Alger County in hopes of logging the land and then selling it for farmland. The area was logged, but it proved to be very poor land for farming.

In 1900, Grand Marais boasted five hotels, two newspapers, thirty saloons, seven clubs, and a population of 3,000. Many of the local residents were of Finnish or Scandinavian origin and were attracted to this area because of the logging boom.

Much of the land within the park boundaries reverted back to the state of Michigan during the 1920s and 1930s due to unpaid taxes. In 1966, the federal government designated 73,653 acres from Munising to Grand Marais as the Pictured Rocks National Lakeshore. The residents of the area looked for a tourist boom that hasn't yet arrived.

Pictured Rocks National Lakeshore

The Pictured Rocks National Lakeshore contains about 15 miles of sandstone cliffs, which rise as high as 200 feet above lake level. The lakeshore also boasts a 12-mile sand beach that connects the Pictured Rocks with the Grand Sable Dunes. The Grand Sable Dunes and Banks are a result of ancient lake, glacial, and wind activity. The banks rise to heights of 275 feet above lake level. Situated on top of the banks are the dunes, which rise an additional 85 feet and cover an area of 5 square miles.

Pictured Rocks is perhaps the most remarkable natural area in the Great Lakes region, with towering cliffs that have been carved out of the shoreline by Lake Superior. Standing on the cliff edge or on the beach, you feel as if nothing humans have made exists between you and the Arctic Circle. The lakeshore supports a variety of wildlife, vegetation, trees, and many water and shore birds. The lakeshore area, with its natural beauty and abundant wildlife, is a nature photographer's paradise.

Beginning in 1988, the U.S. Forest Service and the Pictured Rocks National Lakeshore will have a combined information office in Munising where backcountry permits will be issued. Up to one-third of the backcountry sites can be reserved in advance by writing to: Campground Reservation Request, Pictured Rocks National Lakeshore, P.O. Box 40, Munising, Michigan 49862. If you are short of time before your trip, you can call (906) 387-4697. Remember that peak use of the area occurs in August. Several years ago 14,000 overnights were registered, but in recent years, the totals have been around 9,000. Rangers attribute the earlier volume to national magazine articles that attracted additional visitors.

Recent destruction of live trees for fires has resulted in a rule of no wood fires at Chapel Beach and Mosquito River camping areas. A new campsite, called Potato Patch, has been added and Island View has been dropped. There are now thirteen backcountry campgrounds. In addition, there is a new short trail around Beaver Lake.

Hikers along this linear trail are fortunate to have a shuttle bus service available between mid-June and late September. Current fares and schedules can be obtained by contacting Alger County Public Transportation in Munising, (906) 387-4845.

The visitor center at Munising Falls opens around May 20 and is one place to get your backpacking permit (permits are also available at Pictured Rocks Visitor Information Center in the city of Munising, Park Headquarters at Sand Point, and the information station near Grand Marais). The ranger was exceptionally helpful and had hiked much of the trail. He advised that the section from Sand Point to Miners Castle (3 miles) is wet in the spring and discouraged hiking that section; wet trail conditions are common throughout the area early in the season, so you should ask the ranger about trail conditions. While you are at the falls station, the short walk back to the 75-foot falls is not to be missed. Stepping from the sunny parking lot, you feel the temperature change as you start back and up. The cascading water has carved out the stone, and ferns and other plants somehow manage to maintain their hold on the rocks despite the onslaught.

The park service has completed some extensive construction at the Miners Castle area. The viewing deck and restrooms are striking log structures. The cold updraft from the lake surprises you as you lean over the rail to view the water some 170 feet below. You could leave your car parked here or continue back to the road marked "closed" to park at the Miners Beach area.

There is a spring running down the trail that makes the steep climb from the Miners Beach parking area rather moist. You are rewarded at the top with a big meadow and a lovely falls that runs down the ridge. During the first week in June, the maple leaves are just emerging and the marsh marigolds are blooming. The season is probably three weeks behind the Lower Peninsula. Stop to examine the wild leek that grows profusely along the trail. When stepped on, it gives off a pungent aroma. Camping sites west of Miners Castle are available at Cliffs, which has three individual campsites and one area designated for group camping. The Potato Patch campsite east of Miners Castle has three individual campsites.

The trail continues toward Chapel Beach through a high maple forest with many downed trees. As the trail nears the bluff edge, you can hear the waves crashing far below. We couldn't resist peering over the edge, though the trail itself stays back from the edge. We saw areas where the deer had browsed on young maple trees. The browsing causes a bend or a bow; and these are referred to as staghorn maples.

Off in the distance there are four thin waterfalls running down the sandstone cliff to the lake. The source of the water soon becomes obvious when you come to a wide, marshy stream flowing across the trail and over the edge of the cliff. Some orange markers lead around the marsh; this is the only marking seen. Recent beaver activity caused the flooding. Some distance inland the markings end, and there is no sign of where the marsh ends or where the trail goes. We decided to turn back and later learned from other hikers that they were advised to slog through the stream near the bluff edge to pick up the trail on the other side.

As you walk along the trail to Chapel Beach, you will notice a change in the wind, trees, and temperature; this means you are approaching a steep dropoff beside Chapel Lake. If you continue on down the trail, there is an open area used for camping at Chapel Beach.

In spite of obstacles, visitors have been attracted to Pictured Rocks' grandeur for many generations. A. L. Rawson described his sketching trip to Pictured Rocks for readers of *Harper's* magazine in May, 1867.

One winter evening, many years ago, an Oneida Chief put up at my father's tavern in Central New York, and having been a friend of the family in the East, he was invited to the kitchen, where the great wide-mouthed fireplace warmed his heart and illuminated his countenance, while he astonished and delighted a large circle of listeners, who half neglected their apples and spiced cider listening to the story of his journey to the great West, selecting a new home for his tribe, who were to be removed by the Government at Washington. During that long golden evening I sat snugged up in the corner, swallowing every word, with hair rising and flesh crawling at the thrilling tales; and, when I could take my eyes away from his face long enough, looked among the pictures in the fire for the rocks and waves, bears and deer, panthers and otters, Indians and Canadian voyageurs, wigwams and birch canoes of his (tale). Many times since then I have wished and resolved to see the rocks, the desire has at length been gratified. . . .*

---

*A. L. Rawson, "The Pictured Rocks of Lake Superior," *Harper's New Monthly Magazine* 34, no. 204 (May, 1867): 5–21.

After taking a steamer from Buffalo to Grand Island, Rawson then obtained supplies and guides from Mr. Williams. The party left in a 15-foot boat to visit the rocks.

Here we are at length at the Chapel Beach, and there is the Chapel. Is it not truly named? Like the ruin of some ancient temple, whose roof still rests on a few crumbling columns.

You should take the trail from Chapel Beach around to Grand Portal Point. The trail goes up, down, and around with each hiker seeming to find a separate path through yellow corn lilies. The trip is worth it. Grand Portal Point is truly one of the most spectacular sights the hiker will see in Michigan. The water in the coves is emerald green, with hidden caves, steep cliffs, and water dripping from overhanging cliffs.

Camping areas designated for backpackers occur about every 2 to 4 miles along the trail and so the hiker can somewhat choose whether to make a short day or long day of hiking. After Chapel Beach, the next designated area is Coves.

Farther northeast, the 12-mile Beach Campground and the Hurricane River Campground are both accessible by car. When we drove to the Hurricane River Campground, we encountered the small fly with the big bite. Blackflies can be expected in Pictured Rocks from May through July and sporadically thereafter. One man fishing in the river had obviously been there before. He had on a very handsome homemade net hat. We quickly pulled ours out and proceeded down the two-track toward the Au Sable Point Lighthouse. Here the Park Service is working on exhibits and plans to improve a road and open this area to day visitors. This is an easy walking trail section and would be a nice day hike while camping at the Hurricane River Campground. It is very suitable for the handicapped hiker. The campground was being used largely by retired folks in their pickup campers. We were not impressed with the camp water pump, which was standing in stagnant water.

From Au Sable Point to Logslide is about 3 miles. You have a choice of hiking the water's edge or the crest of the ridge.

On to the Grand Sable area where an old farmhouse,

*Pictured Rocks
National Lakeshore*

the Masse Homestead, has been converted into an information center. Water and outhouses are available here, as well as picnicking and swimming at Grand Sable Lake.

The trail leaves the information area and winds through a maple woods following the course of a stream out to the beach area. Small bridges cross creeks as the trail goes to Sable Falls. From here the hiker can follow the beach to the Grand Marais harbor or County Road H-58 into town, where the local bars provide fresh lake fish and liquid refreshments. Conversation is likely to concern fishing, as many of the local patrons work on fishing boats, or the future of Pictured Rocks.

Conservationists fear the long-term losses of vegetation and wildlife habitat, soil erosion, and the loss of the wilderness character of the area. Will improvements destroy the thing people seek here? We feel that modest improvements are needed.

Porcupine Mountains Wilderness State Park

Trail distance:	80 miles
Terrain:	deep ridges, Great Lakes shoreline
Trail difficulty:	well-marked trails for experienced hikers; some steep elevation changes
Best season:	June through September; some winter access
Governing agency:	DNR
Counties:	Gogebic and Ontonagon

Map on p. 187

The Indians ceded their Ontonagon lands to the United States in 1842. The new state of Michigan did not have funds to build roads or railroads to open the state for settlement and development. This work was accomplished by speculators. One such group got Congress to pass two land grants to enable them to build a ship canal across the Keweenaw Peninsula, giving them altogether 400,000 acres—one half near the line of the proposed canal and the other half from any of the government sections in the Upper Peninsula. Raphael Pumpelly described his work for the Portage Lake and Lake Superior Ship Canal Company in selecting these lands. Beginning in 1866 he sent crews out to evaluate the timber and mineral resources. As you hike in Ontonagon County, you may enjoy recalling Pumpelly's description of how he selected rich pine lands for himself and his employers.

There were no roads but there were a few old Indian trails, and the streams were navigable by bark canoes. The equipment for each party of three to five men was a shelter tent and one or two canoes, a dish pan, a frying pan, tin plates and cups, and each man had an axe and a pair of blankets. The provisions were flour, baking powder, pork, beans, dried fruit, salt, sugar and tea. . . . In the winter months the parties did not carry tents. Even when the thermometer would be far below zero we would spread boughs on the snow and, making a leaning shelter of a blanket which acted like the reflecting surface of a bake oven for the heat of the fire about eight feet in front, we would sleep warm in the dense forest that itself kept off the icy winds.*

Fortunately for hikers today, the remoteness and rugged qualities of the Porcupine Mountains and the unrecognized value of the hardwoods protected the Porcupines. The movement to save the Porkies began in the forties and today 58,332 acres exist as a state park. It contains the largest virgin hardwood-hemlock forest in the United States. The Porcupine Mountains consist of a series of undulating, irregular ranges whose slopes are covered with stands of virgin forest of the hardwood-hemlock type, with maple, birch, and basswood on the upper slopes through hemlock mixtures on the lower areas. Nestled within these ridges are the beautiful Lake of the Clouds and Mirror Lake. From these lakes flow the Big and Little Carp rivers down deep-cut gorges. These rivers rush through a series of rapids and falls to Lake Superior. It is these clean rushing rivers that are the favored habitat for the blackflies.

Entry into the park can be made via County Road 519 to the Presque Isle River Campground on the southwest edge of the park. Another road borders the southern and eastern edges. Most of the numerous hiking trails can be reached via M-107 as it parallels the Superior shore to Lake of the Clouds.

There are thirteen cabins available for rent in the park. These cabins are understandably in demand. They are equipped with pans, dishes, bunks, ax, saw, wood stoves, table, benches, and a broom. Each cabin also has a log book with entries from previous occupants. My limited Spanish vocabulary helped me read one entry only to discover that the cabin occupant tired of solitude and headed to town for a cola. You can reserve one of the cabins by writing in advance to the Park Supervisor, Porcupine Mountains State Park, Route 2, Ontonagon, Michigan 49953. There are two campgrounds that accommodate both tents and trailers, as well as three primitive (tents only) campgrounds.

Bears are reported to be numerous within the park,

---

*James K. Jamison, *This Ontonagon Country: The Story of an American Frontier* (Ontonagon, Mich.: Ontonagon Herald Company, 1939), p. 191.

although we did not see any. The bulletin boards and camp registration offices contain many bear warnings. You are advised to hang your packs 10 feet off the ground and 5 feet from a tree trunk. You will need to bring quite a few feet of nylon rope—about 25 feet per pack in your group. Tie one end of the rope to a small rock or stick and throw that over the selected tree branch. Tie an end to the pack. It will be easier and prevent rope burns if you have a companion lift the pack as you pull on the rope. When securing the end of the rope to the trunk do not use a knot that will tighten itself with the weight of the pack.

Bears are getting smarter, the rangers report. They recognize packs on sight as a source of food; they are no longer dependent only on their noses. Be alert at lunch breaks and keep nothing sweet smelling such as gum or toothpaste in your tent.

Open fires are not permitted. You must carry and use a stove. You must also register, pay for, and carry a backcountry permit. These fees and regulations are helping to maintain the high quality of this area.

This area is Michigan's ultimate high-quality backpacking area; it is large and beautiful, with 80 miles of well-marked trail options to happily occupy you for a week or longer. The hikes described here are only a few of the combinations possible. The rangers at campgrounds will be happy to advise you on trail choices, muddy areas, and which direction to hike the steeper trails—this last item can make a big difference in your enjoyment and in the time it takes to reach your destination. Park rangers shared with us the many changes that have been made to the hiking trail system in the Porcupine Mountains. We are excited about the park managers' interest in enhancing the backpacking experience, as demonstrated by these changes.

Hikers wanting to explore the interior of the park will want to park at Summit Peak Road. The road has been improved with a parking area added. A new trail, Beaver Creek Trail, has been added. It begins at Summit Peak Road and travels to the Little Carp Trail. The trail includes a bridge over the Little Carp River and a boardwalk over adjacent marshland. This new trail will offer much to naturalists, bird watchers, and those interested in trailside fishing.

About 3 miles of the Big Carp Trail that were very muddy have been repaired and rerouted. The new trail section located along the base of the Miscowabic and LaFayette peaks winds through open stands of hemlock and mature hardwoods. The new section offers excellent hiking and is very scenic.

Sections of the Little Carp River Trail have been rerouted because of damage caused by a very large flood in 1983. Hikers will encounter numerous river crossings along this trail and a new section along the river.

It is easy to combine a longer backpacking loop with a few days of day hiking on shorter trails. Our first was a day hike to Lily Pond. From the parking area on Little Carp River Road, you cross a board bridge over the Little Carp River to begin the 2½-mile hike to the Lily Pond. The next stream crossing was made on slippery logs. This is very pleasant hiking with short uphill and downhill sections on well-marked trail. There are a few muddy spots to hop around and very limited spots to stop and take a break.

If it is near lunch time, you might want to hike all the way to the Lily Pond where there is a wooden bridge to sit on and catch a good breeze. If you wait quietly you might catch a glimpse of a member of the beaver family whose dwelling is about 15 feet away. You might also ask to borrow the rowboat from the rental cabin to row across to the spring to get fresh water. A sign will direct you to the water.

The Lily Pond Trail would be a good start for a leisurely loop around Mirror Lake or it can be the start of a week-long trip. It is only one of many starting points and loop possibilities within the park.

The Presque Isle River picnic grounds is the start of the longest trail in the park, the Lake Superior Trail, which is 16 miles. You begin by crossing over the Presque Isle River on a swinging suspended cable bridge. At the waterfall you can feel the power of the river as it joins Lake Superior. The beach here would be good swimming on a hot day for masochists willing to submit their bodies to water that is never warm. The Lake Superior Trail does not follow the shoreline until it reaches Little Carp River cabin.

The Government Peak Trail loop starts from a small

parking lot on M-107. The trail starts up a rocky incline. It is a well-marked trail within a hemlock-hardwood forest. We then climbed another hill with a view through the hemlocks to the cascading Carp River inlet. Two miles in there is a bench where the Union Spring Trail joins. This would be a good planned rest stop. There is a bench also at Trap Falls. The 15-foot falls spreads out across a rocky ledge. This section of trail has red clay soil, rocks, and a lot of tree roots to trip you.

A sign points the way to the Adirondack shelter, which was much nicer than we expected. There are three other trailside shelters in the park. The enclosure of the fourth side with screening provided protection from bugs while providing a view and sounds of the rushing stream. Inside we found signs of previous occupation by porcupines. Fortunately we spotted them before turning in or their nighttime gnawing under the cabin might have caused us some anxious moments. The nighttime temperature dropped to 32°, and our impression was that a tent would have been warmer.

You will follow the trail uphill when you leave the shelter the next morning. The trail goes through mature maples with ferns and young maples in the understory. It is well marked with a lot of uphill and downhill sections. About 2 miles down the trail you will come across a side trail that goes up Government Peak.

At the top of the peak there is a picnic table. Take time to walk over to the north edge of the peak and you can look out over the valley to Lake Superior. It's worth doing to get a view of the horizon after being in the heavy underbrush. The trail down the west side of the peak is in better condition and shows signs of recent maintenance.

From here you could hike the short section of North Mirror Lake Trail to the lake where there are numerous pleasant places to set a tent. There are two cabins at the lake. The stream by the larger cabin provides clean water that is easier to get than water from the lake, which has mushy edges. We borrowed a rowboat to get a view of the area. Some people were fishing but no one was swimming. When the temperature at suppertime is 45°, you turn in early.

Heading the opposite way, the Mirror Lake Trail has a

long descent as you head north. This is the direction the ranger recommended. It is taxing on the knees but there are benches along the way to rest on. The trail parallels a creek for a while and then goes through an area with an open understory. When you cross the wooden bridge near Lake of the Clouds you can hear voices from the overlook above and you are five minutes from another resting bench. This break will prepare you for the climb up the steep escarpment. Don't stop long for you will appreciate the lake much more from above. The trail is very steep but you can climb it quickly. When you get near the top, a sign points to the right and says M-107 is 4 miles. Go left and you will reach the overlook and parking area in about five minutes. From the overlook you can see where you have been and be amazed. You can take time to sun on the rocks, take pictures, and find someone to ride back to your car with, or you can continue along the Escarpment Trail.

The view from the overlook is outstanding, unmarred in any direction by man-made scars. The impresssion is that here we did it right. It is a wonderful impression to have as you leave the Porkies.

Sylvania Recreation Area

Trail distance:	30 miles
Terrain:	glacial lakeland
Trail difficulty:	easy to moderate
Best season:	April through mid-October
Governing agency:	Ottawa National Forest
Public transit:	Greyhound Bus Lines
County:	Gogebic

Map on p. 188

This land was bought in the early 1900s by officials of the United States Steel Corporation for a hunting and fishing club. Their shares were later sold to William Boyce Thompson, a copper mine magnate. Thompson's son-in-law, Anthony Drexel Biddle, Jr., a former United States ambassador to Poland, had a log cabin built on a bay on Clark Lake. No ordinary cabin, this one was 240 feet long and contained seventeen bedrooms and an indoor tennis court. Biddle died without ever using the cabin. The logs from the cabin were sold at auction after the Forest Service purchased the area for five million dollars.

Fishermen have been the primary users of this 21,000-acre area in the Ottawa National Forest. The key feature and attraction is the many large and small lakes created in the depressions glaciers left behind. The waters are clear and of high quality because the lakes are situated on the Mississippi/Lake Superior divide, so there is no inlet to supply nutrient matter to the lakes. Special fishing regulations exist in Sylvania. Only artificial lures may be used. No largemouth or smallmouth bass may be kept, and special size limits apply to lake trout, walleye, and northern pike.

A trail constructed by the Youth Conservation Corps has made this a more interesting area for a backpacker. Clark Lake Trail is a 7-mile trail around the largest of

Sylvania's lakes. This trail allows the backpacker to hike to all six campsites on that lake and also gives access to several other lakes with connecting trails. Also located on Clark Lake is an immaculate sandy swimming beach.

When hiking the 7-mile trail we at first wondered why the trail followed all of the indentations and points of the shoreline. As soon as the trail went inland, we found our answer. When the shore breeze is lost, the increase in mosquitoes is significant. Head nets are very helpful while hiking, setting up camp, and cooking.

The trails are marked with blue paint blazes. The addition of trails along the shore will decrease the privacy of some camp areas although more than half of the campsites can be reached only by canoes and some only by portaging the canoe from one lake to another.

There are conveniently located water pumps at parking areas and in the center of the area which make it possible to refill canteens. The lake water can also be treated and used. Campfires are permitted and there is an ample supply of deadwood lying on the ground. A small backpacking saw and a little work would allow you to build a fire to cook your 30-inch fish.

Camping is carefully regulated. Visitors are assigned to a camp area. Each named camp area consists of three sites, each of which has a designated tent area, table, and metal fire circle. The three sites share an outhouse. The camping regulations are helping to minimize the impact of people on the area and you will see the difference between Sylvania and areas where people are allowed to camp willy-nilly.

The Sylvania Visitor Center in Watersmeet has exhibits, a color slide show, and wonderful restrooms. You can get your camping permit there or at the Visitor Information Center located on County Road 535, some 5 miles southwest of Watersmeet.

There are approximately 20 miles of trail within the area. It would be suitable for a week or less. You will probably set up camp in one or two sites and then do some day hiking, swimming, and exploring. You might also plan to combine canoeing and fishing with day hiking.

ADDITIONAL RESOURCES

Information Resources

Accommodations and Transportation

Michigan's tourist facilities are distributed throughout the state because of the extensive number of streams, rivers, lakes, and forests. For planning a trip to a new area, you may want to consult one of the following organizations.

Southeast Michigan Travel and Tourist Association
64 Park St., Box 1590
Troy, Michigan 48099

East Michigan Tourist Association
One Wenona Park
Bay City, Michigan 48706

West Michigan Tourist Association
136 Fulton East
Grand Rapids, Michigan 49502

Upper Peninsula Travel and Recreation Association
P.O. Box 400
Iron Mountain, Michigan 49801

They will provide you with maps, lists of accommodations, festivals, and interesting places to visit.

It is possible to take a bus to within 10 miles of many of the trails described in this book. To get a complete schedule contact your local Greyhound or Indian Trails offices.

As you plan your Michigan backpacking trip you will have a choice of accommodations along the way ranging from primitive forest service campgrounds to the Grand Hotel on Mackinac Island. Try the Grand's Sunday brunch for a royal treat. Numerous camping opportunities exist within the national parks, forests, and lakeshores as well as state parks and forests and in private campgrounds. The following addresses provide accesss to information about them.

National Parks
Isle Royale National Park.   Isle Royale was the first of

Michigan's national parks, established in 1940. In addition to camping, there is one inn on the island, which can be welcome at the beginning or end of a hike. Write to the Park Superintendent, Isle Royale National Park, 87 N. Ripley St., Houghton, Michigan 49931. The Superintendent can supply you with current information about the inn as well as the latest boat and plane schedules.

There are four options for transportation to the island.

1. The *MV Ranger III* carries 125 passengers from Houghton to Rock Harbor. Contact Isle Royale National Park, Houghton, Michigan 49931, (906) 482-0984.
2. The *Isle Royale Queen* goes from Copper Harbor to Rock Harbor. Contact Isle Royale Ferry, Copper Harbor, Michigan 49918, (906) 482-4950.
3. The ferry from Grand Portage, Minnesota, is operated by Isle Royale Transportation Line, Inc., 366 Lake Ave. S., Duluth, Minnesota 55802 (218) 722-0945.
4. Or try a float plane, the *Sky Ranger,* which flies daily from Houghton to Rock Harbor and Windigo. Contact Isle Royale Seaplane Service, P.O. Box 371, Houghton, Michigan 49931, (906) 482-8850.

Pictured Rocks National Lakeshore. There are three established campgrounds in addition to backcountry camps. For information, contact the Park Superintendent, Pictured Rocks National Lakeshore, Munising, Michigan 49862.

Sleeping Bear Dunes National Lakeshore. Established in 1970, this is the newest of Michigan's national parks. Information may be obtained from the Park Superintendent, Sleeping Bear Dunes National Lakeshore, 400½ Main St., Frankfort, Michigan 49635.

Transportation to South Manitou Island may be arranged by contacting Manitou Island Transit, Box 605, Leland, Michigan 49654, (616) 256-9061.

National Forests

National forests are under multiple-use management, and in most areas they permit hunting, logging, mining, and motorized vehicles, as well as camping and hiking. They have many small primitive camping areas with pumps and pit toilets, and you are also permitted to camp in backcountry areas. The headquarters of the three national forests in Michigan are:

Ottawa National Forest
P.O. Box 468
Ironwood, Michigan 49938

Hiawatha National Forest
Post Office Building
Escanaba, Michigan 49829

Huron-Manistee National Forest
421 South Mitchell St.
Cadillac, Michigan 49601

State Parks
The camping areas range in size from twenty-five to five hundred sites. From Memorial Day to Labor Day many of the popular parks are full. Fees are charged. Up to 50 percent of the sites can be reserved by payment of a reservation fee. To obtain information or reservations, write to Parks Division, Department of Natural Resources, P.O. Box 30028, Lansing, Michigan 48909.

State Forests
Most state forest areas have primitive campgrounds. Fees are now charged at all campgrounds. For information contact the Forest Management Division, Department of Natural Resources, P.O. Box 30028, Lansing, Michigan 48909.

Private Campgrounds
You will find a listing of these in the *Rand McNally Eastern Campground and Trailer Parks* guide. This guide also lists federal and state campgrounds and gives road directions to all of them.

Other Map Sources
Another helpful book to guide you to your trailhead, campground, or accommodation is the book of county maps published by the Michigan United Conservation Clubs. It is found in some bookstores or can be ordered from the club at P.O. Box 2235, Lansing, Michigan 48911. County maps may sometimes be obtained from local DNR headquarters or county road commissions.

Mail Order Equipment Suppliers

A letter to one of the suppliers listed here will bring you catalogs for years. These can be used to compare prices, weights, and test data. We have listed those that we have personally ordered equipment from.

L. L. Bean, Inc.
Freeport, Maine 04033

Campmor
810 Route 17 N.
P.O. Box 997-F
Paramus, New Jersey 07653

Early Winters, Ltd.
110 Prefontaine Place S.
Seattle, Washington 98104

Marmot Mountain Works
331 S. 13th
Grand Junction, Colorado 81501

Recreational Equipment Inc.
P.O. Box c-88125
Seattle, Washington 98140

Michigan Groups That Promote Trails and Hiking

American Youth Hostels
Metropolitan Detroit Council
3024 Coolidge
Berkley, Michigan 48072

Michigan Trailfinders
2680 Rockhill Dr. N.E.
Grand Rapids, Michigan 49505

North Country Trail Association
P.O. Box 311
White Cloud, Michigan 49349

Sierra Club
Mackinac Chapter
115 West Allegan, Suite 10-B
Lansing, Michigan 48933

Other Books You May Enjoy

Barker, Harriet. *Supermarket Backpacker.* Chicago: Contemporary Books, 1977.

Barnes, Burton V., and Wagner, Warren H., Jr. *Michigan Trees: A Guide to the Trees of Michigan and the Great Lakes Region.* Ann Arbor: University of Michigan Press, 1981.

Bradt, G. W., and Schafer, Charles E. *Michigan Wildlife Sketches.* Hillsdale, Mich.: Hillsdale Educational Publishers, 1971.

Bull, John. *The Audubon Society Field Guides to North American Birds: Eastern Region.* New York: Alfred A. Knopf, 1977.

Bunnelle, Hasse, *Food for Knapsackers and Other Trail Travellers.* San Francisco: Sierra Club Books, 1971.

Bunnelle, Hasse, and Sarvis, Shirley. *Cooking for Camp and Trail.* San Francisco: Sierra Club Books, 1972.

Cantor, George. *The Great Lakes Guidebook: Lake Huron and Eastern Lake Michigan.* New ed. Ann Arbor: University of Michigan Press, 1985.

————. *The Great Lakes Guidebook: Lake Superior and Western Lake Michigan.* Ann Arbor: University of Michigan Press, 1980.

DuFresne, Jim. *Isle Royale National Park: Foot Trails and Water Routes.* Seattle: Mountaineers, 1984.

Fleming, June. *The Well-Fed Backpacker.* New York: Random House, 1981.

Fletcher, Colin. *The Complete Walker III.* 3d ed. New York: Alfred A. Knopf, 1984.

Hart, John. *Walking Softly in the Wilderness.* Rev. ed. San Francisco: Sierra Club Books, 1984.

Hendrickson, Gerth E. *The Angler's Guide to Ten Classic Trout Streams in Michigan.* Ann Arbor: University of Michigan Press, 1985.

Hubbs, Carl L., and Lagler, Karl F. *Fishes of the Great Lakes Region.* Ann Arbor: University of Michigan Press, 1964.

Kjellstrom, Bjorn. *Be Expert with Map and Compass: The Orienteering Handbook.* Rev. ed. New York: Charles Scribner's Sons, 1976.

Klots, Elsie B. *The New Field Book of Freshwater Life.* New York: G. P. Putnam's Sons, 1966.

Manning, Harvey. *Backpacking: One Step at a Time.* 3d ed. New York: Random House, 1980.

Information Resources

Maye, Patricia. *Fieldbook of Nature Photography.* San Francisco: Sierra Club Books, 1974.

Michigan County Maps and Outdoor Guide. Lansing: Michigan United Conservation Clubs, 1977.

Niering, William A., and Olmstead, Nancy C. *The Audubon Society Field Guide to North American Wildflowers.* Including Eastern Region. New York: Alfred A. Knopf, 1979.

Rand McNally's Campground and Trailer Park Guide. New York: Rand McNally & Co., 1986.

The Sierra Club Guide to the National Parks East and Middle West. New York: Random House, 1986.

Sierra Club Naturalist's Guide to the North Woods of Michigan, Wisconsin, Minnesota and Southern Ontario. San Francisco: Sierra Club Books, 1981.

Simonds, Roberta L., and Tweedie, Henrietta H. *Wild Flowers of the Great Lakes Region.* Chicago: Chicago Review Press, 1984.

Smith, Alexander H., and Weber, Nancy Smith. *The Mushroom Hunter's Field Guide: All Color and Enlarged.* Ann Arbor: University of Michigan Press, 1980.

Smith, Norman F. *Michigan Trees Worth Knowing.* 5th ed. Hillsdale, Mich.: Hillsdale Educational Publishers, 1978.

Wilkerson, James A., ed. *Medicine for Mountaineering.* 3d ed. Seattle: Mountaineers, 1985.

Opportunities for Handicapped Backpackers

Michigan has trails of varying types and difficulty, enabling hikers, whether disabled or not, to choose the trails most suited for them. Because of Jerry's experience backpacking as a handicapped hiker, we are including these suggestions and sources of information.

First, the question is not whether a handicpaped person can or cannot have the experience of outdoor adventure, but whether he or she is willing to try and to accept the risk that it might not be easy or completely comfortable. Once that is accepted, then there are really two optional beginnings. One is to join an organized group program sponsoring river rafting, skiing, horseback riding, camping, or hiking trips. The other option is to backpack with family and friends.

Backpacking involves camping activities and some form of mobility. It isn't a competitive sport; speed and distance are less important than the pleasure one gains. Some trial and error is involved for everyone. Jerry started using a frame backpack and later found that an internal frame pack worked best for him. We have included sources of special equipment. Also, contact local rehabilitation agencies for addresses of local or regional companies that can modify artificial prosthetic devices as well as equipment for the handicapped hiker. Experiments with equipment can begin in the backyard and then move on to car camping and day hiking. Many state parks have facilities accessible to wheelchairs.

Equipment

American Foundation for the Blind
Consumer Products Department
15 West 16th St.
New York, New York 10011

They sell a Braille compass made by Silva and other special equipment; catalog available.

Organizations

Minnesota Outward Bound School
308 Walker Ave., S.
Wayzata, Minnesota 55391

Outward Bound has an adventure program for the disabled including canoeing, camping, hiking, backpacking, and map and compass work.

North American Riding for
the Handicapped Association
P.O. Box 100
Ashburn, Virginia 22011

Environmental Traveling Companions
Fort Mason, Building 312
San Francisco, California 74123
(415) 474-7662

They organize rafting trips on the American River in northern California.

Publications

Michigan Department of Natural Resources
P.O. Box 30028
Lansing, Michigan 48909
Handicapped Facilities in Michigan State Parks

National Easter Seal Society for
Crippled Children and Adults
2023 W. Ogden Ave.
Chicago, Illinois 60612
Directory of Resident Camps for Persons with Special Needs

ACCESS
Consumer Information Center
Pueblo, Colorado 81009

Write for their 200-page book, *Access National Parks: A Guide for Handicapped Visitors,* which includes Michigan's National Parks. It is available in some libraries.

MAPS

1. Allegan
2. Beaver Island
3. Green Pine Lake
4. High Country
5. Hoist Lakes
6. Jordan River
7. Shore to Shore
8. Muncie Lakes
9. Nordhouse Dunes
10. North Country
11. Sand Lakes
12. Sleeping Bear Dunes
13. Waterloo-Pinckney
14. Bay de Noc—Grand Island
15. Bruno's Run
16. Cedar River
17. Craig Lake
18. Fox River
19. Isle Royale
20. McCormick Tract
21. Natural Area
22. North Country
23. Pictured Rocks
24. Porcupine Mts.
25. Sylvania

LOWER PENINSULA
TRAIL MAPS

Beaver Island ●
● Shore to Shore
Jordan River
Sleeping Bear Dunes ● ● ● High Country
Shore to Shore ● ● Sand Lakes
Muncie Lakes ●
● Hoist Lake
Shore to Shore ●
Shore to Shore ●
Nordhouse Dunes ●
● Green Pine Lake
● North Country
● Allegan
● Waterloo–Pinckney

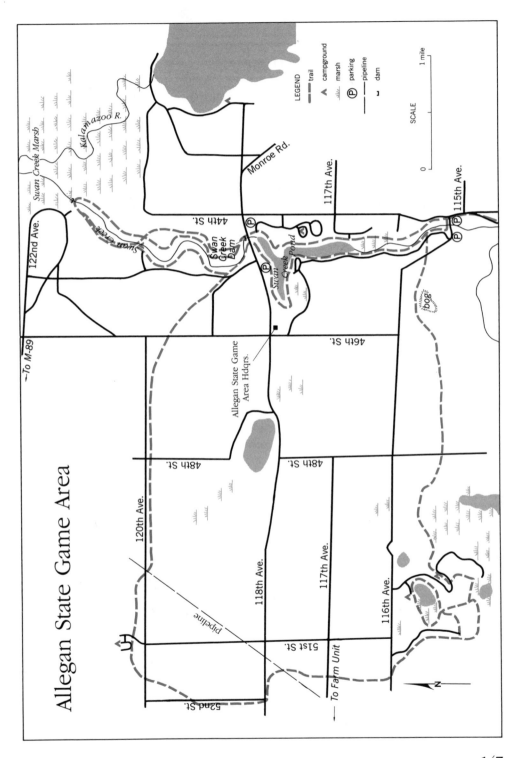

Allegan State Game Area

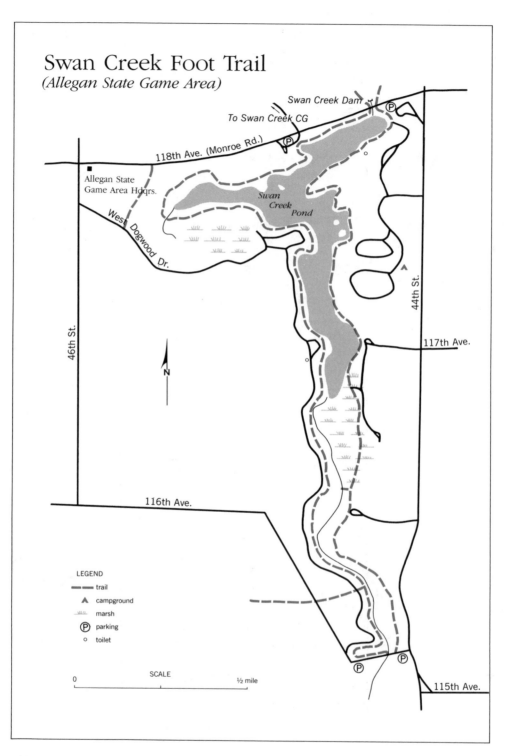

Swan Creek Foot Trail
(Allegan State Game Area)

Swan Creek Dam

To Swan Creek CG

118th Ave. (Monroe Rd.)

Allegan State
Game Area Hdqrs.

West Dogwood Dr.

Swan
Creek
Pond

44th St.

46th St.

117th Ave.

116th Ave.

LEGEND

trail

campground

marsh

parking

toilet

SCALE

0

½ mile

115th Ave.

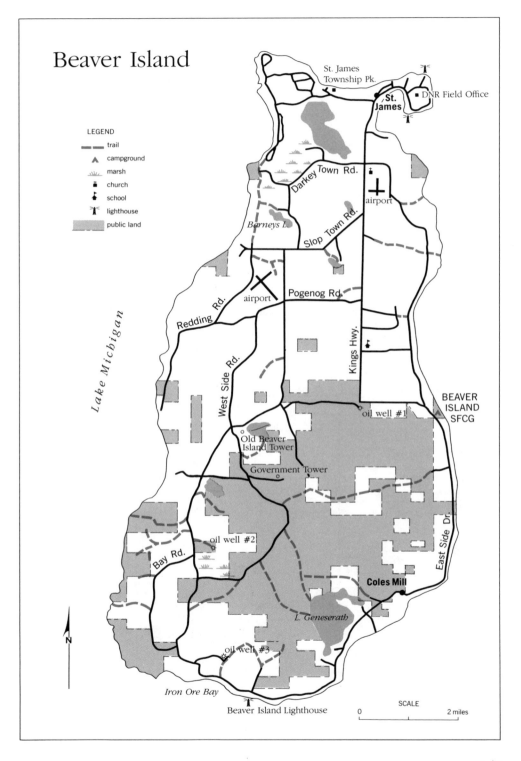

Beaver Island

LEGEND
- – – – trail
- ⋀ campground
- marsh
- ■ church
- ♟ school
- ⅄ lighthouse
- public land

St. James
Township Pk.

■ DNR Field Office

St. James

Darkey Town Rd.

airport

Slop Town Rd.

Barneys L.

Lake Michigan

X airport

Redding Rd.

Pogenog Rd.

West Side Rd.

Kings Hwy.

oil well #1

BEAVER ISLAND SFCG

○ Old Beaver Island Tower

Government Tower ○

Bay Rd.

oil well #2

East Side Dr.

Coles Mill

oil well #3

L. Geneserath

N

Iron Ore Bay

⅄
Beaver Island Lighthouse

SCALE

0   2 miles

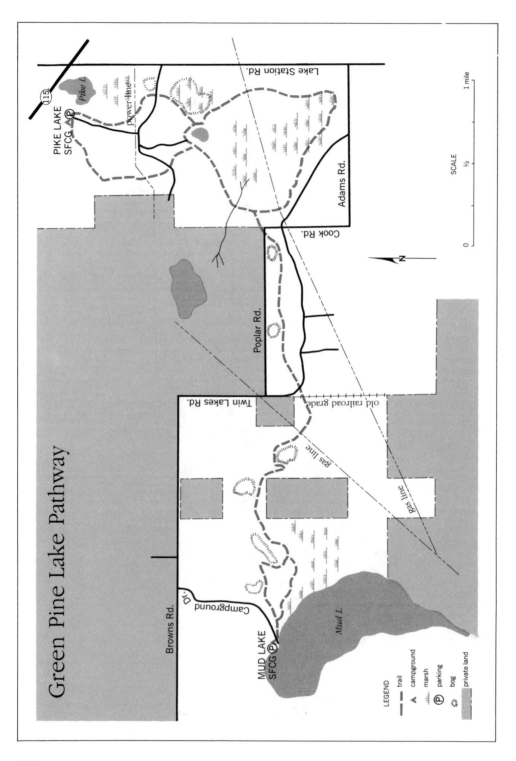

Green Pine Lake Pathway

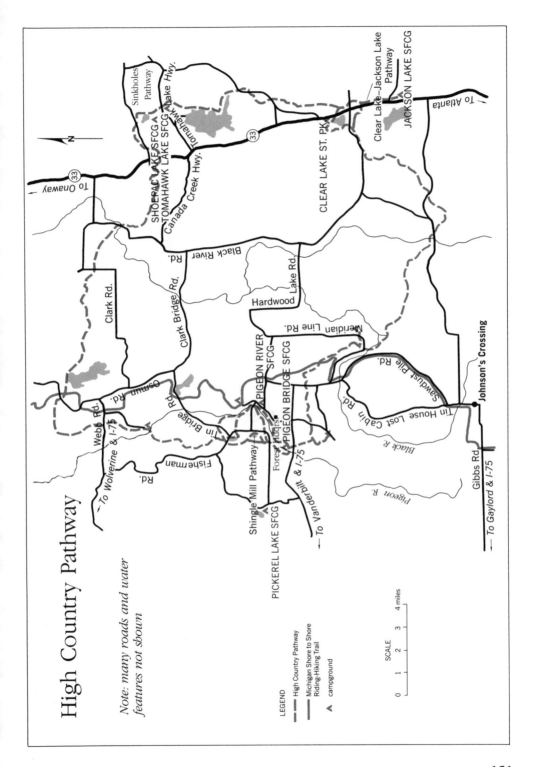

High Country Pathway

Note: many roads and water features not shown

LEGEND

High Country Pathway

Michigan Shore to Shore
Riding-Hiking Trail

▲ campground

SCALE

0 1 2 3 4 miles

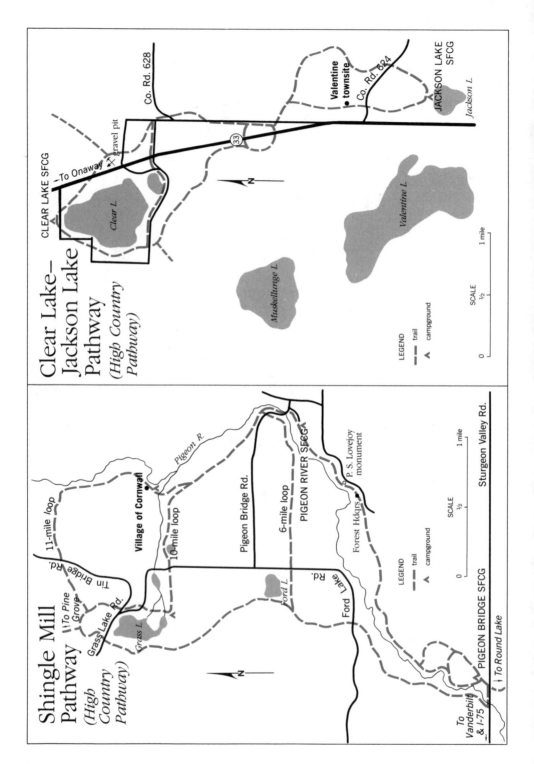

Clear Lake–
Jackson Lake
Pathway
*(High Country
Pathway)*

Co. Rd. 628

gravel pit

—To Onaway

CLEAR LAKE SFCG

Clear L.

33

Valentine
townsite

Co. Rd. 624

JACKSON LAKE
SFCG

Jackson L.

N

Valentine L.

Muskellunge L.

LEGEND
- - - trail
▲ campground

SCALE
0   ½   1 mile

Shingle Mill
Pathway
*(High
Country
Pathway)*

Pigeon R.

11-mile loop

Tin Bridge Rd.

To Pine Grove

Grass Lake Rd.

Grass L.

Village of Cornwall

10-mile loop

Pigeon Bridge Rd.

6-mile loop

Ford L.

Ford Lake Rd.

PIGEON RIVER SFCG

P. S. Lovejoy
monument

Forest Hdqrs.

N

LEGEND
- - - trail
▲ campground

SCALE
0   ½   1 mile

PIGEON BRIDGE SFCG

Sturgeon Valley Rd.

To Round Lake

To
Vanderbilt
& I-75

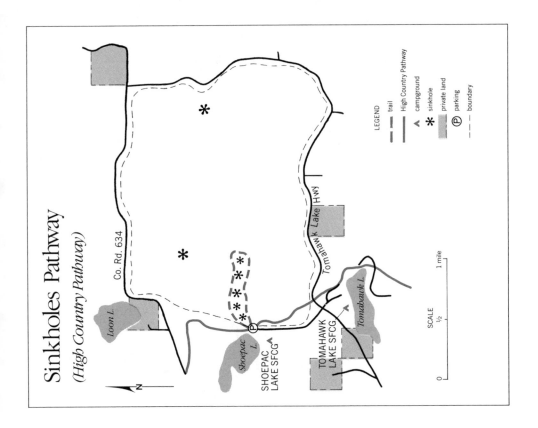

Sinkholes Pathway
(High Country Pathway)

LEGEND

- — — trail
- ■ High Country Pathway
- ◄ campground
- ✳ sinkhole
- ▨ private land
- Ⓟ parking
- – – boundary

SCALE

0   ½   1 mile

Hoist Lakes Foot Travel Area

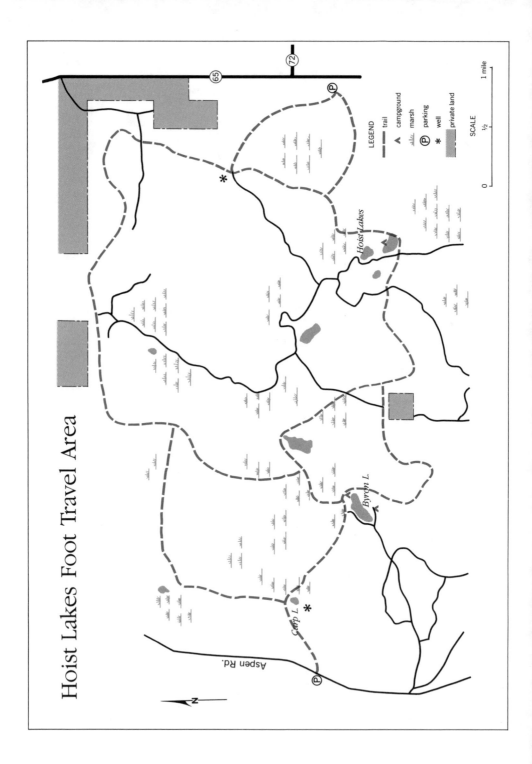

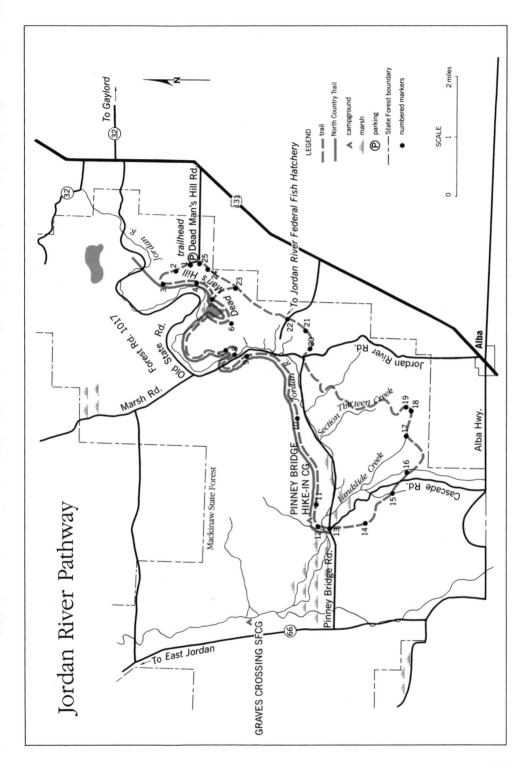

Jordan River Pathway

LEGEND

- trail
- North Country Trail
- ▲ campground
- marsh
- ⓟ parking
- State Forest boundary
- ● numbered markers

SCALE

0   1   2 miles

N

To Gaylord

To Jordan River Federal Fish Hatchery

Dead Man's Hill Rd.

trailhead

Dead Man's Hill

Jordan R.

Old State Rd.

Forest Rd. 1017

Marsh Rd.

Mackinaw State Forest

Jordan R.

Section

Thirteen Creek

Landslide Creek

Jordan River Rd.

Cascade Rd.

Alba Hwy.

Alba

PINNEY BRIDGE HIKE-IN CG

Pinney Bridge Rd.

GRAVES CROSSING SFCG

To East Jordan

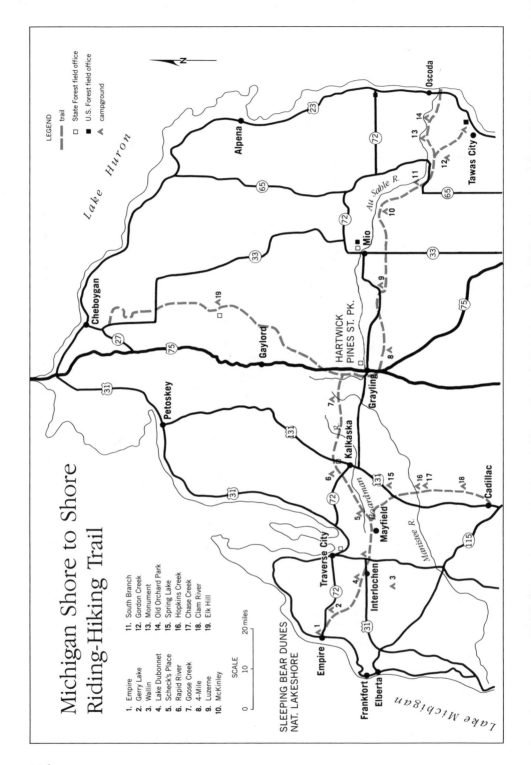

Michigan Shore to Shore
Riding-Hiking Trail

1. Empire
2. Gerry Lake
3. Wallin
4. Lake Dubonnet
5. Scheck's Place
6. Rapid River
7. Goose Creek
8. 4-Mile
9. Luzerne
10. McKinley
11. South Branch
12. Gordon Creek
13. Monument
14. Old Orchard Park
15. Spring Lake
16. Hopkins Creek
17. Chase Creek
18. Clam River
19. Elk Hill

LEGEND

trail
☐ State Forest field office
■ U.S. Forest field office
⋀ campground

SCALE

0   10   20 miles

SLEEPING BEAR DUNES
NAT. LAKESHORE

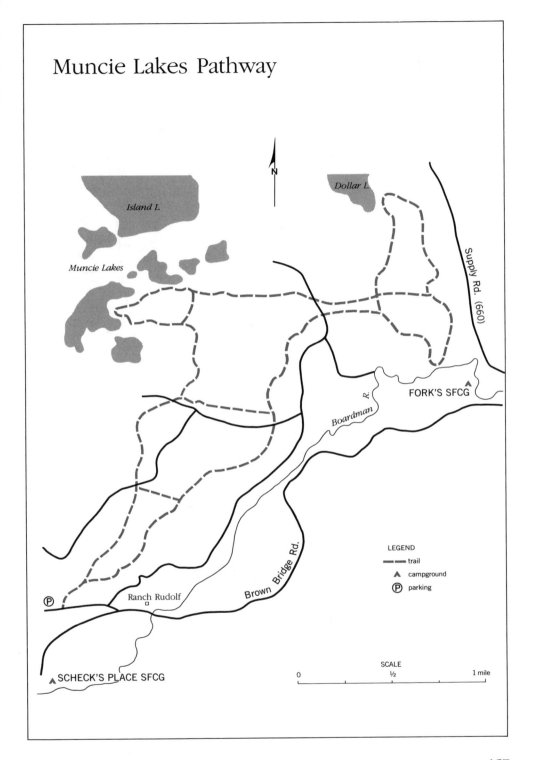

Muncie Lakes Pathway

Island L.

Dollar L.

Muncie Lakes

Supply Rd. (660)

Boardman R.

FORK'S SFCG

LEGEND

— — trail

▲ campground

Ⓟ parking

Ⓟ

Ranch Rudolf

Brown Bridge Rd.

SCALE

0   ½   1 mile

▲ SCHECK'S PLACE SFCG

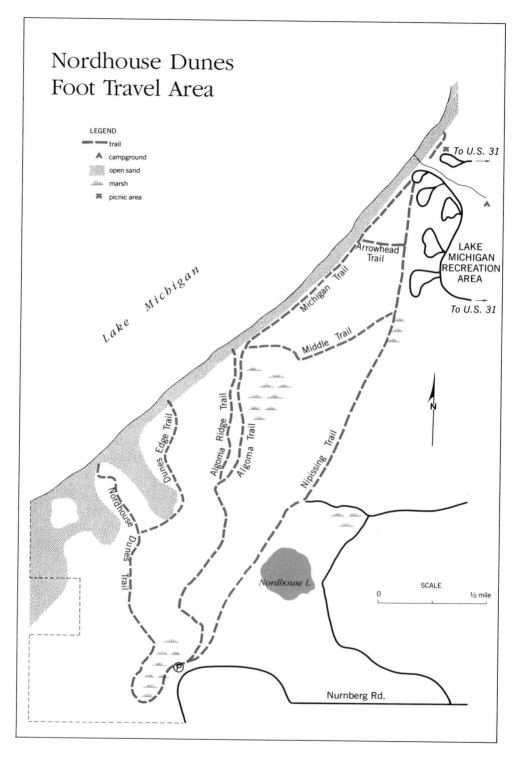

Nordhouse Dunes
Foot Travel Area

LEGEND
- - - - trail
▲ campground
░░ open sand
~ marsh
🏕 picnic area

Lake Michigan

Arrowhead Trail

Michigan Trail

Middle Trail

Dunes Edge Trail

Algoma Ridge Trail

Algoma Trail

Nipissing Trail

Nordhouse Dunes Trail

🏕 To U.S. 31

▲

LAKE MICHIGAN RECREATION AREA

To U.S. 31

N

Nordhouse L.

SCALE

0   ½ mile

P

Nurnberg Rd.

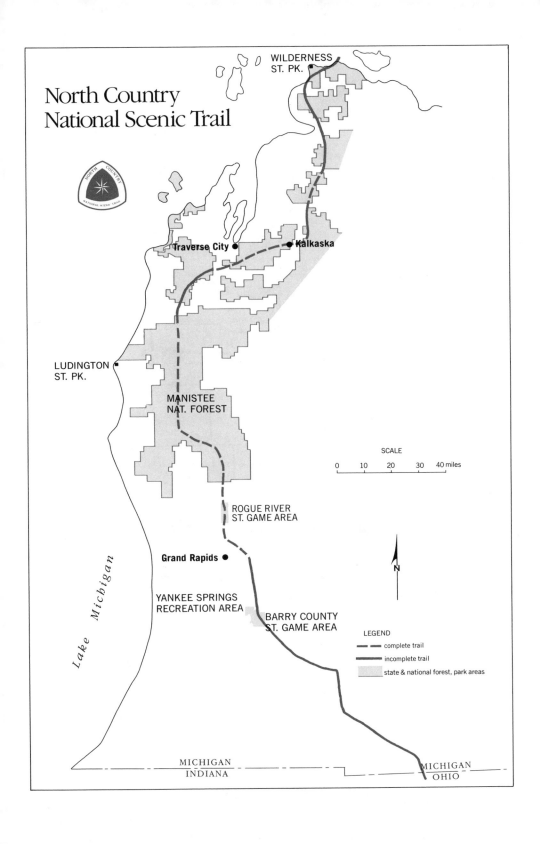

North Country
National Scenic Trail

WILDERNESS
ST. PK.

Traverse City ● ● Kalkaska

LUDINGTON
ST. PK.

MANISTEE
NAT. FOREST

SCALE

0   10   20   30   40 miles

ROGUE RIVER
ST. GAME AREA

Grand Rapids ●

N

Lake Michigan

YANKEE SPRINGS
RECREATION AREA

BARRY COUNTY
ST. GAME AREA

LEGEND

━ ━ complete trail

━━━ incomplete trail

▨ state & national forest, park areas

MICHIGAN
INDIANA

MICHIGAN
OHIO

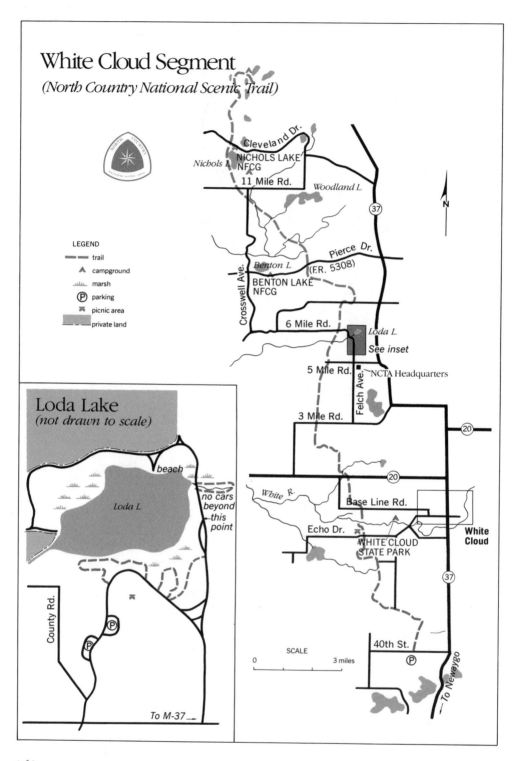

White Cloud Segment
(North Country National Scenic Trail)

Cleveland Dr.

Nichols L.

NICHOLS LAKE
NFCG

11 Mile Rd.

Woodland L.

37

LEGEND
- ▬ ▬ trail
- ▲ campground
- marsh
- Ⓟ parking
- ⚞ picnic area
- private land

Pierce Dr.

Benton L.

(F.R. 5308)

BENTON LAKE
NFCG

Crosswell Ave.

6 Mile Rd.

Loda L.

See inset

5 Mile Rd.

NCTA Headquarters

Felch Ave.

3 Mile Rd.

20

Loda Lake
(not drawn to scale)

beach

no cars
beyond
this
point

Loda L.

White R.

20

Base Line Rd.

Echo Dr.

WHITE CLOUD
STATE PARK

White
Cloud

County Rd.

⚞

Ⓟ

Ⓟ

37

SCALE

0   3 miles

40th St.

Ⓟ

To Newaygo

To M-37

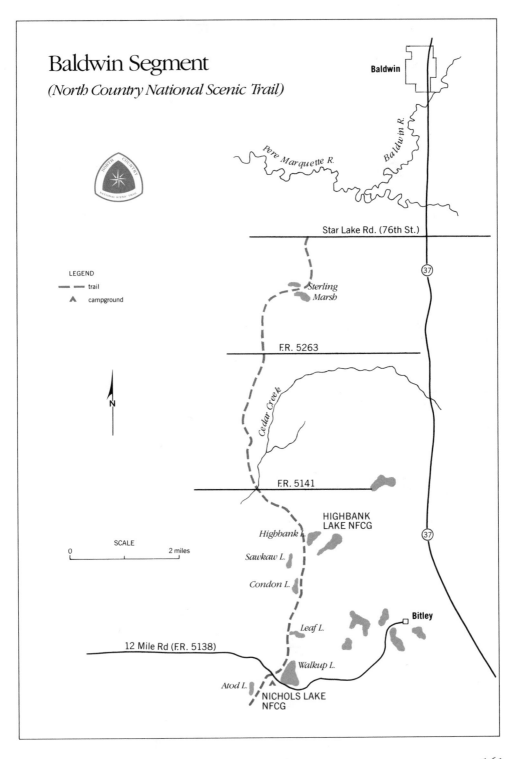

Baldwin Segment

(North Country National Scenic Trail)

Baldwin

Baldwin R.

Pere Marquette R.

Star Lake Rd. (76th St.)

37

Sterling
Marsh

F.R. 5263

Cedar Creek

N

F.R. 5141

HIGHBANK
LAKE NFCG

Highbank L.

SCALE

0   2 miles

Sawkaw L.

Condon L.

Bitley

Leaf L.

12 Mile Rd (F.R. 5138)

Walkup L.

Atod L.

NICHOLS LAKE
NFCG

37

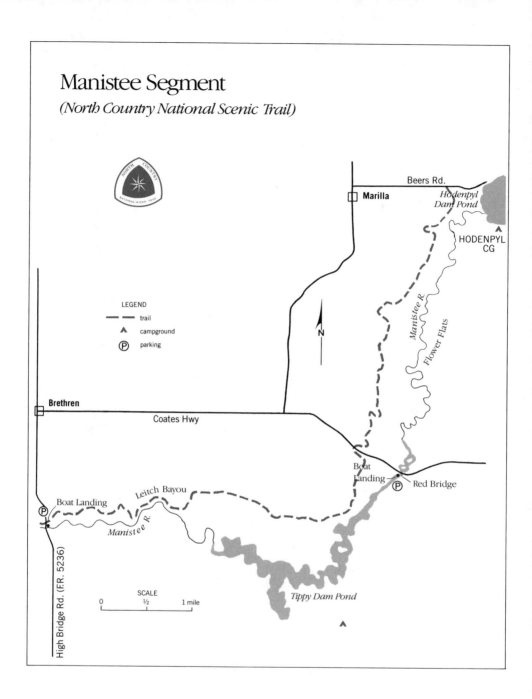

Manistee Segment

(North Country National Scenic Trail)

LEGEND
- – – – trail
- ▲ campground
- Ⓟ parking

Beers Rd.

Marilla

Hodenpyl Dam Pond

HODENPYL CG

Manistee R.

Flower Flats

N

Brethren

Coates Hwy

Boat Landing — Red Bridge

Boat Landing

Leitch Bayou

Manistee R.

High Bridge Rd. (F.R. 5236)

SCALE
0   ½   1 mile

Tippy Dam Pond

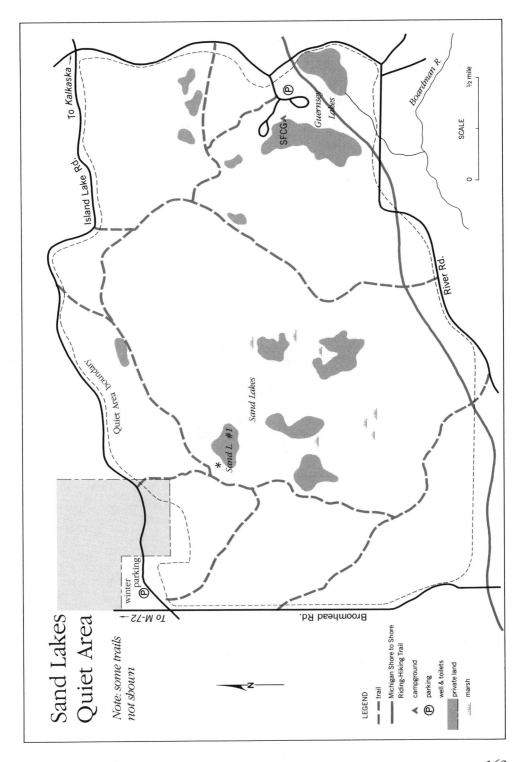

Sand Lakes Quiet Area

Note: some trails not shown

To Kalkaska

Island Lake Rd.

Guernsey Lakes

SFCG

Boardman R.

SCALE

0   ½ mile

River Rd.

Quiet Area Boundary

Sand Lakes

Sand L. #1

*

winter parking

To M-72

Broomhead Rd.

N

LEGEND

trail

Michigan Shore to Shore Riding-Hiking Trail

campground

P   parking

well & toilets

private land

marsh

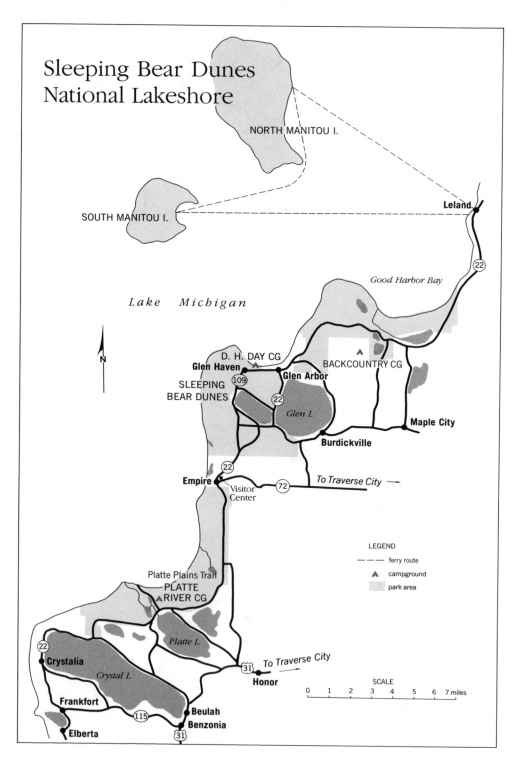

Sleeping Bear Dunes
National Lakeshore

NORTH MANITOU I.

SOUTH MANITOU I.

Leland

Good Harbor Bay

Lake   Michigan

N

D. H. DAY CG

BACKCOUNTRY CG

Glen Haven

Glen Arbor

109

SLEEPING
BEAR DUNES

22

Glen L.

Maple City

Burdickville

22

Empire

Visitor
Center

72

To Traverse City →

LEGEND

– – –   ferry route

▲   campground

park area

Platte Plains Trail
PLATTE
RIVER CG

Platte L.

22

Crystalia

To Traverse City →

31

Crystal L.

Honor

SCALE

Frankfort

0   1   2   3   4   5   6   7 miles

115

Beulah

Benzonia

Elberta

31

Platte Plains Trails

(Sleeping Bear Dunes National Lakeshore)

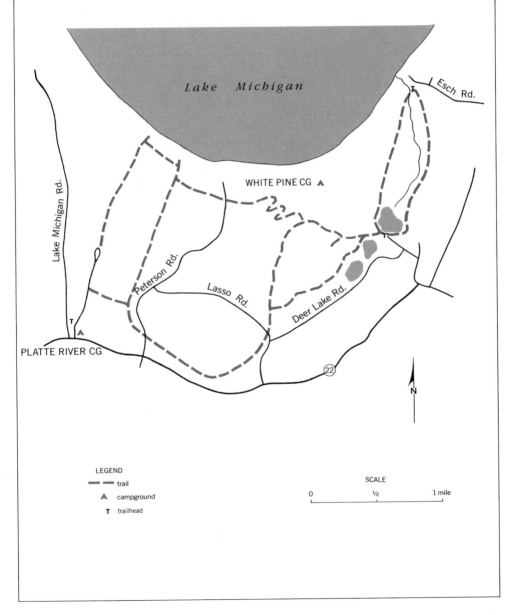

Lake Michigan

Esch Rd.

WHITE PINE CG ▲

Lake Michigan Rd.

Peterson Rd.

Lasso Rd.

Deer Lake Rd.

PLATTE RIVER CG

22

N

LEGEND

▬ ▬ trail

▲ campground

T trailhead

SCALE

0   ½   1 mile

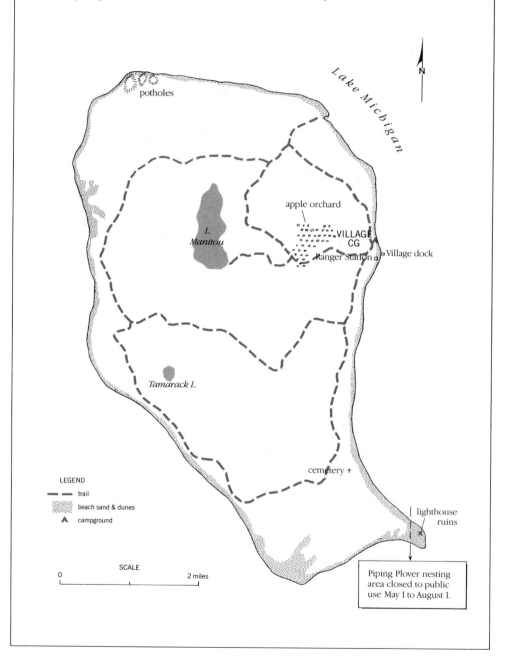

North Manitou Island

(Sleeping Bear Dunes National Lakeshore)

Lake Michigan

N

potholes

apple orchard

L. Manitou

VILLAGE CG

Ranger Station ▫ ▫ Village dock

Tamarack L.

cemetery +

LEGEND

— — trail

beach sand & dunes

▲ campground

SCALE

0   2 miles

lighthouse ruins

Piping Plover nesting area closed to public use May 1 to August 1.

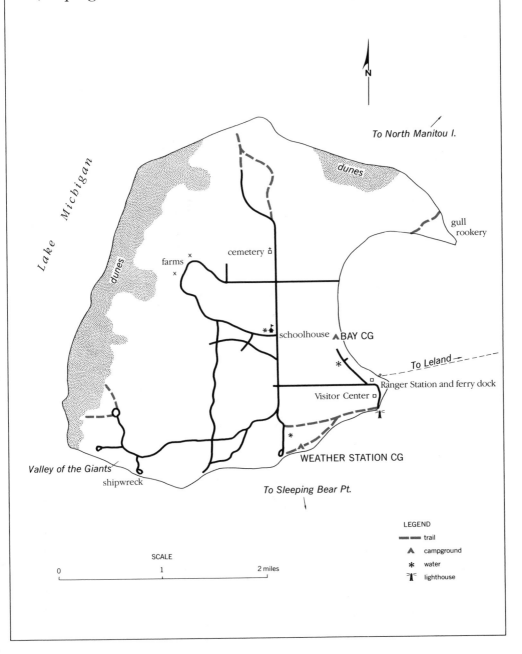

South Manitou Island

(Sleeping Bear Dunes National Lakeshore)

N

Lake Michigan

To North Manitou I.

dunes

gull
rookery

dunes

farms ×
×

cemetery ▯

*★ schoolhouse ▲ BAY CG

*

To Leland

Ranger Station and ferry dock

Visitor Center ▯

Valley of the Giants
shipwreck

* WEATHER STATION CG

To Sleeping Bear Pt.

LEGEND

━ ━ trail
▲ campground
★ water
⚓ lighthouse

SCALE

0   1   2 miles

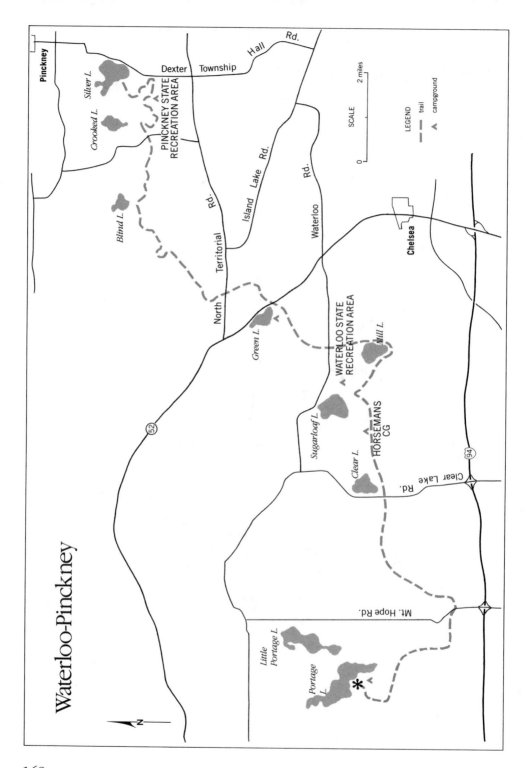

Waterloo-Pinckney

UPPER PENINSULA
TRAIL MAPS

Isle Royale

Porcupine Mts.

North Country

Craig Lake

McCormick Tract

Sylvania

Pictured Rocks

Natural Area

Fox River

Bruno's Run

Bay de Noc–Grand Island

North Country

Cedar River

Bay de Noc–Grand Island Trail

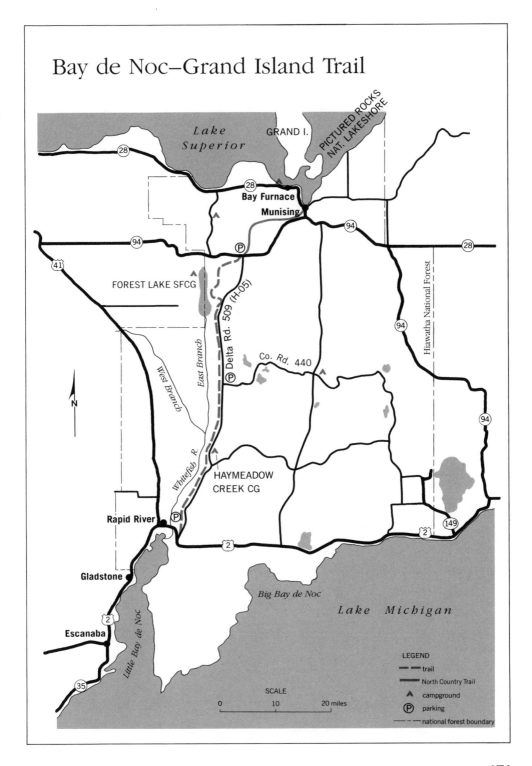

LEGEND

- – – – trail
- ▬ ▬ North Country Trail
- ▲ campground
- Ⓟ parking
- – · – national forest boundary

SCALE

0   10   20 miles

Bruno's Run

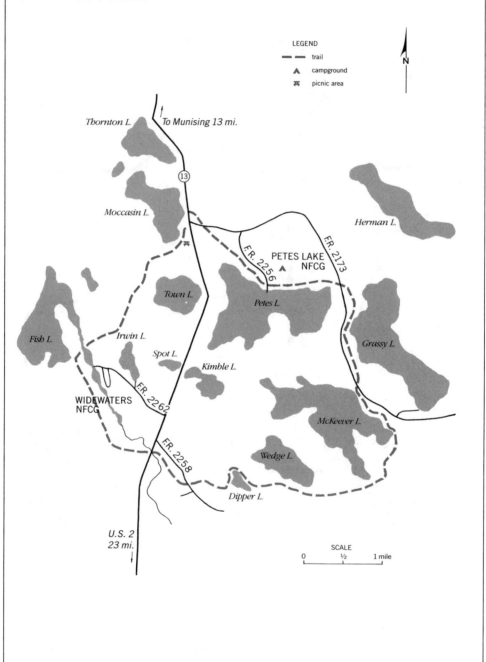

LEGEND
- – – trail
- ▲ campground
- 🎪 picnic area

N

Thornton L.

To Munising 13 mi.

⑬

Moccasin L.

Herman L.

F.R. 2256

PETES LAKE
NFCG

F.R. 2173

Town L.

Petes L.

Fish L.

Irwin L.

Grassy L.

Spot L.

Kimble L.

WIDEWATERS
NFCG

F.R. 2262

McKeever L.

F.R. 2258

Wedge L.

U.S. 2
23 mi.

Dipper L.

SCALE
0   ½   1 mile

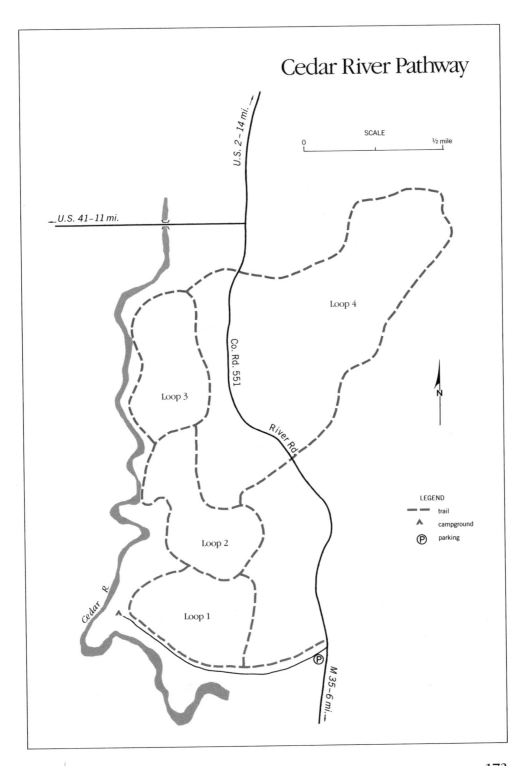

Cedar River Pathway

SCALE

0 — ½ mile

U.S. 2 – 14 mi.

U.S. 41 – 11 mi.

Co. Rd. 551

River Rd.

Loop 4

Loop 3

Loop 2

Loop 1

Cedar R.

M 35 – 6 mi.

N

LEGEND

- - - trail

▲ campground

Ⓟ parking

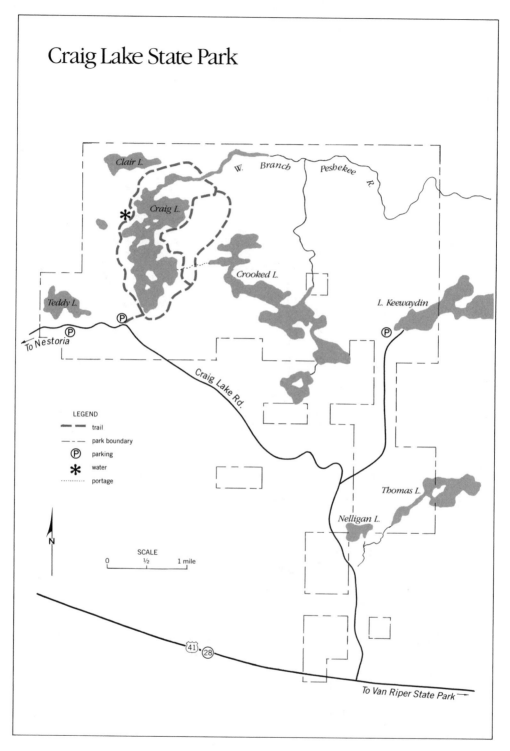

Craig Lake State Park

Clair L.

Craig L.

W. Branch Peshekee R.

Teddy L.

Crooked L.

L. Keewaydin

To Nestoria

Craig Lake Rd.

LEGEND

- — — — trail
- — · — park boundary
- Ⓟ parking
- ✳ water
- ·········· portage

N

SCALE

0   ½   1 mile

Thomas L.

Nelligan L.

41 · 28

To Van Riper State Park →

174   UPPER PENINSULA

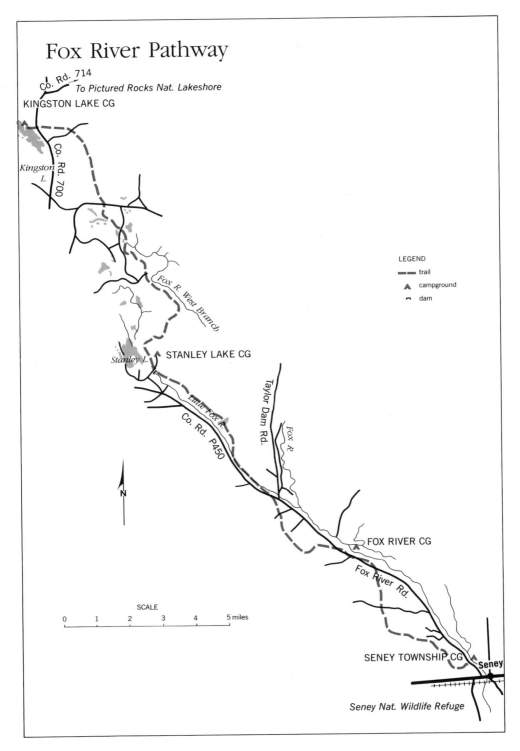

Fox River Pathway

Co. Rd. 714
To Pictured Rocks Nat. Lakeshore
KINGSTON LAKE CG

Kingston L.

Co. Rd. 700

LEGEND

— — trail

▲ campground

⌐ dam

Fox R. West Branch

Stanley L. STANLEY LAKE CG

Taylor Dam Rd.

Fox R.

Little Fox R.

Co. Rd. P450

N

▲ FOX RIVER CG

Fox River Rd.

SCALE

0   1   2   3   4   5 miles

SENEY TOWNSHIP CG **Seney**

Seney Nat. Wildlife Refuge

Isle Royale National Park

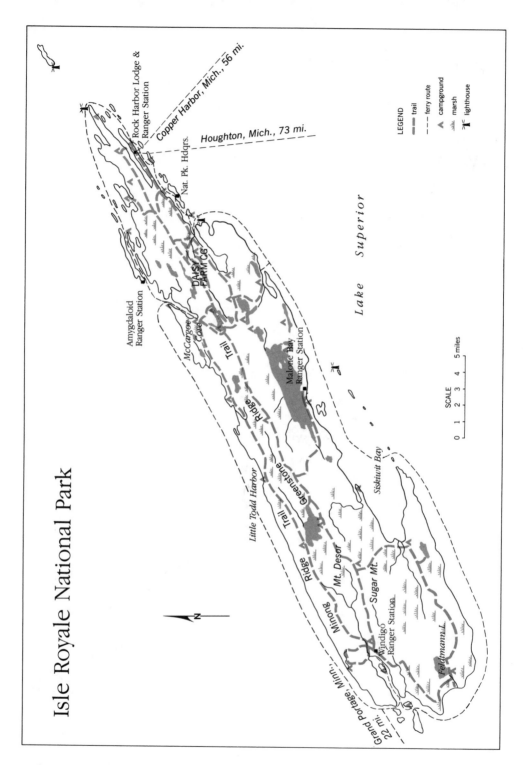

UPPER PENINSULA

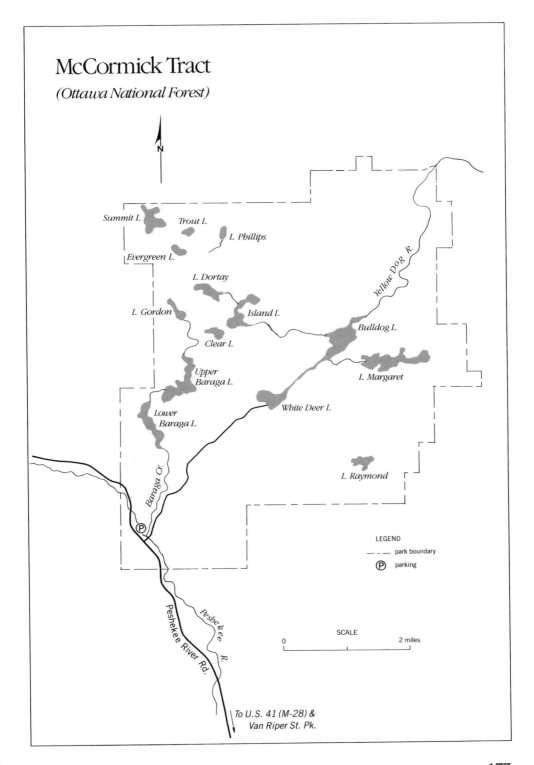

McCormick Tract
(Ottawa National Forest)

N

Summit L.

Trout L.

L. Phillips

Evergreen L.

L. Dortay

L. Gordon

Island L.

Clear L.

Bulldog L.

Upper
Baraga L.

L. Margaret

Lower
Baraga L.

White Deer L.

Yellow Dog R.

Baraga Cr.

L. Raymond

LEGEND

— · — park boundary

Ⓟ parking

Peshekee River Rd.

Peshekee R.

SCALE

0   2 miles

To U.S. 41 (M-28) &
Van Riper St. Pk.

Natural Area
Pathway

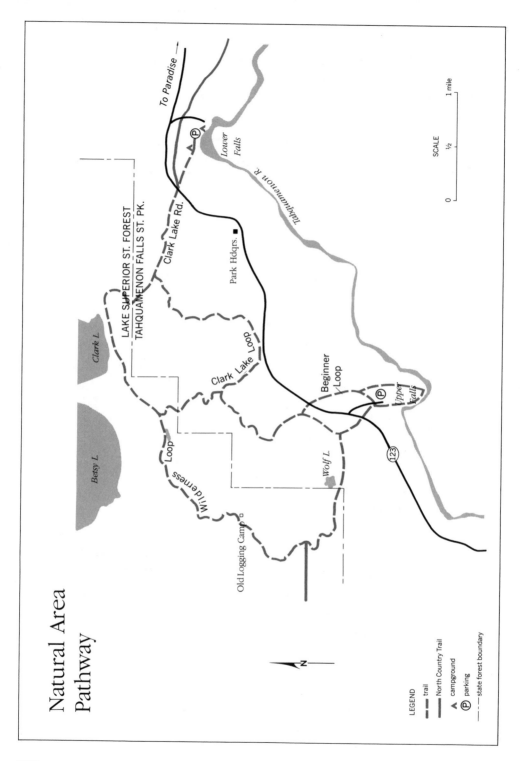

North Country National Scenic Trail

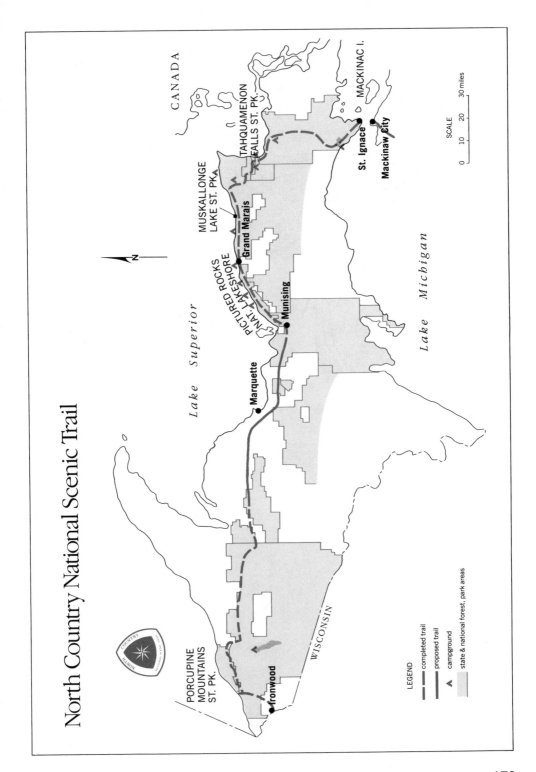

CANADA

Lake Superior

Lake Michigan

WISCONSIN

PORCUPINE
MOUNTAINS
ST. PK.

Ironwood

Marquette

Munising

PICTURED ROCKS
NAT. LAKESHORE

Grand Marais

MUSKALLONGE
LAKE ST. PK.

TAHQUAMENON
FALLS ST. PK.

St. Ignace

MACKINAC I.

Mackinaw City

N

SCALE

0   10   20   30 miles

LEGEND

— — — completed trail

——— proposed trail

▲ campground

state & national forest, park areas

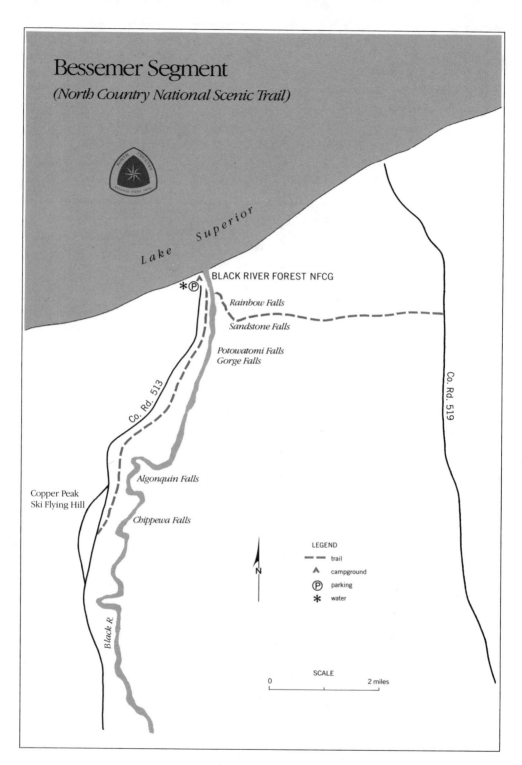

Bessemer Segment
(North Country National Scenic Trail)

Lake Superior

BLACK RIVER FOREST NFCG

Rainbow Falls

Sandstone Falls

Potowatomi Falls
Gorge Falls

Co. Rd. 513

Co. Rd. 519

Algonquin Falls

Copper Peak
Ski Flying Hill

Chippewa Falls

Black R.

N

LEGEND
– – – trail
▲ campground
Ⓟ parking
✳ water

SCALE
0   2 miles